A *Business Week* Guide
Small Business
Trends and
Entrepreneurship

The Editors of *Business Week*

McGraw-Hill, Inc.
New York   San Francisco   Washington, D.C.   Auckland   Bogotá
Caracas   Lisbon   London   Madrid   Mexico City   Milan
Montreal   New Delhi   San Juan   Singapore
Sydney   Tokyo   Toronto

Library of Congress Cataloging-in-Publication Data

A Business week guide : small business trents and entrepreneurship   /
    the editors of Business week.
        p.   cm.
    Includes index.
    ISBN 0-07-009424-1 (alk. paper)
        1. Small business.   2. Entrepreneurship.   I.   Business week (New
York, N.Y.)   II.   Title: Small business trends and entrepeneurship.
    HD2341.B876   1995
    658.02′2—dc20   94-32878
                                                                              CIP

1 2 3 4 5 6 7 8 9 0   DOC/DOC   9 0 9 8 7 6 5 4

ISBN 0-07-009424-1

*The sponsoring editor for this book was Philip Ruppel, the editing supervisor
was Paul R. Sobel, and the production supervisor was Donald F. Schmidt. It
was set in Palatino by McGraw-Hill's Professional Book Group composition
unit.*

Printed and bound by R. R. Donnelley & Sons Company.

A *Business Week* Guide
Small Business Trends and Entrepreneurship

Other *Business Week* Guides Published by McGraw-Hill

Contents

Preface   vii

Introduction: How Entrepreneurs Are Shaping the
Economy and What Businesses Can Learn   ix

Part 1. Small Is Powerful

1. Just What Is an Entrepreneur?   3

2. Meet the Giant Killers   11

Part 2. The New Economies of Scale

3. Technology—Start with Some High-Tech
   Magic   21

4. Management—Belt-Tightening the Smart
   Way   29

5. Marketing—How to Get Closer to Your
   Customers   35

6. Finance—The Floodgates Inch Open   43

7. Finance—Lenders to the Small Fry   49

Part 3. Techniques and Trends

8. Letting Go Is Hard to Do   55

9. Turning Rivals into Teammates   61

10. How Goliaths Can Act like Davids   67

11. Entrepreneurship around the World   75

12. Small Business and the Japanese
    Experience   81

13. Percy Barnevik's Global Crusade at ABB   87

14. Jack Welch on the Art of Thinking Small   93

15. Women Entrepreneurs: They're Forming
    Small Businesses at Twice the Rate of Men   99

16. Business Week/Harris Executive Poll: What's
    Worrying Small Business   107

17. Self Test: How Entrepreneurial Is Your
    Company?   111

Index   117

Preface

In contemplating a topic for a bonus issue of *Business Week* in 1993, we realized that the upheavals in Corporate America were not isolated events. Companies as disparate as IBM, General Motors, Westinghouse, and American Express—long were encountering problems that, in some cases, threatened their very existence. Bigness, once considered essential for success, was becoming a liability for many companies. They just didn't seem capable of moving fast enough to deal with a rapidly evolving world economy. Nor could they cope with massive technological shifts. More and more, it seemed that smaller, nimbler competitors were outclassing the titans—in everything from retailing to high tech.

The successes posed some questions. Yes, the entrepreneurial spirit was clearly more evident in small business than in Corporate America. But why? And why were smaller companies, lacking resources and economics of scale, able to do what bigger companies couldn't?

Yet at the same time, there were obvious exceptions. Somehow, GE, AT&T, Motorola, and other giants were able to transform themselves, to take on the same sort of entrepreneurial energy that characterized a Wal-Mart, an Intel, a Microsoft, or even a start-up. What was it that enabled these giants to change when others couldn't?

Intriguing questions, all. We knew, of course, that there were no easy generalizations, no how-to-do it formulas. So we decided these questions would form the basis of an indepth examination of the quality we call enterprise. The result was an issue of the magazine that was itself a sterling example of enterprise in action—the drive, energy, and imagination of a dedicated group of editors combined with the resources that a big, international magazine can summon to the task. More that 100 of our editors participated in the project.

Based on the success of the issue, we and our sister company, McGraw-Hill Professional Books, decided to join forces and produce this book, A *Business Week Guide: Small Business Trends and Entrepreneurship*. As with our other books such as *The Quality Imperative, Business Week's Guide to Mutual Funds*, and *Business Week's Guide to the Best Business Schools*, we believe this will be a valuable resource.

Stephen B. Shepard
Editor-in-Chief
Business Week

Introduction: How Entrepreneurs Are Shaping the Economy and What Businesses Can Learn

What astonishes me in the United States is not so much the marvelous grandeur of some undertakings as the innumerable multitude of small ones.

Alexis de Tocqueville, 1835

What the peripatetic Frenchman noticed nearly 160 years ago—before the advent of Apple Computer, Genentech, Microsoft, or Nucor—is just as true today. The only difference is that the spirit of enterprise is more than ever a global phenomenon with few bounds.

From the rows of kiosks selling goods on nearly every block in Moscow to the cramped factories in Taiwan, Russian *biznezmen* and Chinese *changshang* are reshaping their nations' economies in much the same way as those ingenious old

Yankees created the basis for America's business culture just after independence was won.

Any modern-day de Tocqueville would notice something else about this global shift: Changes in the rules of the business game are putting a premium on the entrepreneurial qualities of small companies. Today's successful enterprises are nimble, innovative, close to the customer, and quick to market. They're not bureaucratic, centrally controlled institutions that are slow to change. It adds up to a new management catechism with many of the hallmarks of small business.

In recent years, the giants of industry have suffered a great comeuppance—as much from the little guys as from fierce global competition. IBM continues to reel from the assaults of erstwhile upstarts such as Microsoft, Dell Computer, and Compaq Computer. Big Steel was devastated by such minimills as Nucor, Chaparral Steel, and Worthington Industries. Onetime mavericks Wal-Mart Stores and The Limited taught Sears, Roebuck a big lesson. Southwest Airlines has profitably flown through turbulence that has caused the big airline carriers to rack up $10 billion in losses over the past three years. And a brash pack of startups with such names as Amgen Inc. and Centocor Inc. has put the U.S. ahead in biotechnology—not Bristol-Myers Squibb, Merck, or Johnson & Johnson.

Sure, some industries, such as auto making and petrochemicals, still require size and scale. But the swift pace of technological change and the fragmentation of markets are eroding the traditional economies of scale. Indeed, some management thinkers now speak of the "diseconomies of scale," the unresponsiveness, sluggishness, and high costs that come with bureaucracy. While the behemoths try to adjust to new competitive realities, younger and smaller companies have emerged as the agents of change in economies around the world.

Although there is some disagreement over the exact numbers, most observers agree that entrepreneurs are generating more jobs and more innovation than the giants. In the U.S., small and midsize companies created all of the 5.8 million new jobs from 1987 to 1992—at a time when companies with 500 or more employees recorded a net loss of 2.3 million jobs, according to Cognetics Inc., a Cambridge (Mass.) research firm. This year, small business is expected to generate an additional 1.7 million jobs, while companies with 25,000 or more employees will shed 300,000 people. And despite their more limited resources, one recently published study shows that small companies also produce 2.4 times as many innovations as large outfits.

As John. F. Welch Jr., chairman of General Electric Co., puts it: "Size is no longer the trump card it once was in today's brutally competitive world marketplace—a marketplace that is unimpressed with logos and sales numbers but demands, instead, value and performance." His goal in managing $60 billion-plus GE: To "get that small-company soul—and small-company speed—inside our big-company body."

What Welch and so many other chieftains of big enterprise are trying to do is tap what might be called the economies of entrepreneurship. Xerox Corp. deploys a venture fund to bankroll internally generated ideas that previously were discarded or overlooked. The chief executive of MCI Communications Corp.—now a $10 billion company—appears on a closed-circuit TV network to give impassioned talks on the merits of entrepreneurship. PepsiCo Inc., hoping to get all its employees acting like small-business owners, dishes out stock options to janitors and secretaries.

And U.S. companies aren't the only ones trying to tap the wellsprings of entrepreneurship. Philips Electronics, the $31 billion European giant, for example, is allowing employees to pitch new ideas to a committee of top executives responsible for funding and approval, much as an entrepreneur would bring an idea to a venture capitalist. Why? Philips found that lower-level managers, worried about budgets or other projects, often blocked new ideas. "We're bringing top decision-makers to bear on new ideas so something terrific doesn't die on the vine," says Frank P. Carubba, a Philips executive vice-president.

The debate over whether smaller companies are more productive than bigger ones is itself causing a sea change in attitudes and management thinking. These days, it seems, most big companies appear intent on acting small. Ironically, of course, most small companies continue to spend a lot of their time trying to become big, especially because bigness still symbolizes success.

As long as corporations around the world continue to downsize, however, the entrepreneurship movement is likely to accelerate. Indeed, the trend away from vertical integration is leading more big companies to subcontract and outsource more and more products and services from smaller companies. And the dynamism of small business is being discovered across the globe as nations reject central planning for capitalist models. "The U.S. is now focusing more on the importance of entrepreneurship and away from its reliance on large corporations and government for economic development," says James L. Freeley, a management professor and board member of the Foundation for Economic Literacy, an educational effort to help Russians understand the benefits of capitalism. "Russia's only hope is entrepreneurship and small business. Not only did they never have large private corporations but the state-operated entities and military complexes are being rapidly phased out."

While Russia is only now rediscovering the virtues of small business, the entrepreneur has had a largely unbroken run as a celebrated figure in American culture. The coopers, farmers, silversmiths, and other artisans of Colonial times were the forebears of the scrappy startups in today's economy. "From the time of Thomas Jefferson to the present, many Americans have seen the owners of small businesses as epitomizing all that is best about the American way of life," says Mansel G. Blackford, a business historian at Ohio State University.

Until the late 19th century, small companies were the norm. But the entrepreneur was much diminished during the subsequent rapid industrialization of America. Big Business rose to ascendancy in fields where economies of scale were critical to success: railroads, steel, autos, chemicals, and telephones.

In this century, the postwar economy favored Big Business for more than four decades. The share of business receipts going to small companies—those with fewer than 500 employees or less than $5 million in sales—fell from 52% to just 29% of the total for all American companies between 1958 and 1979.

But these boom years also led to complacency, flab, and decline for many of the giants of industry. "Big businesses still keep people in narrow organizational boxes, doing work that does not matter, pushing paper that no one wants, and allowing little room for creativity and fun," says Craig J. Cantoni, author of *Corporate Dandelions* and president of Capstone Consulting

Group in Scottsdale, Ariz. That prevailing view of the lumbering giants of business helped the entrepreneur make a comeback at the start of the 1980s. Apple Computer Inc.'s Steve Jobs and People Express Airlines Inc.'s Donald Burr became cult heroes to new generations.

Now, fast-changing competition, advances in technology, and changes in the marketplace are combining to make the environment ever more difficult for large corporations. The reason: These changes are erasing many of the costly entry barriers that protected Big Business from pesky startups. "The capital advantage big companies sometimes have is being eliminated," says Ted Stolberg, a venture capitalist who invests in small companies. "The technology is helping smaller companies beat up the big guys."

A decade ago, for example, it took a $20 million to $30 million investment to gain the precision and efficiency to make mechanical parts that today can be made on a flexible machining center that sells for $500,000 to $1.5 million. Computing power that 10 years ago cost hundreds of thousands of dollars and was available only to large, resource-rich corporations can now be put on a desktop for a few thousands bucks. Overnight delivery services such as Federal Express Corp. and United Parcel Service Inc. have mushroomed, all but eliminating the need for costly warehouse and distribution centers. And the willingness of more companies to join with others in strategic alliances to produce and sell products makes it easier than ever to compete in nearly any market.

Nor do larger research and development budgets and expanded staffs guarantee that big companies can bring new products to market faster than smaller ones. Why? "The key people in small businesses are closer to the customer, so they're more in tune with what's happening in the marketplace," says Nancy C. Pechloff, managing director of Arthur Andersen & Co.'s Enterprise Group, a consulting practice for small businesses. "In large companies, a lot of lower-level employees may be coming up with the ideas, but they often don't have the power to make them happen."

No less important, creative people tend to gravitate to entrepreneurial environments that offer more independence and flexibility. "The raw material that goes into small business is more innovative," Pechloff believes. "The process of big companies turns creative people off."

Of course, the vast majority of small businesses around the world lead a modest, often precarious existence. Many of them go belly-up within a couple of years. Precious few of them propel their leaders to the forefront. But difficult as it can be, there is something compelling about life as the founder of a business. "Entrepreneurs are obsessed with creating value," says Thomas D. Weldon, chief executive officer of Novoste Corp., a medical products company in Norcross, Ga. "It's extremely satisfying to build something from nothing. Risk puts the edge on it. If there isn't the possibility of failure, you don't jump over tall buildings in a single bound."

Once they cut their ties to large corporations, few entrepreneurs look back. Typical of them is Ken Sharma, who co-founded Intellection Inc., a Dallas-based software concern, in 1989. He had worked for Texas Instruments Inc. for 15 years, rising to become manager of information systems and services. "I was a company man," Sharma says. "I learned to claw my way up. But I realized that the power given to me by others was no power at all. What the small company gives me is the ability to do something meaningful and to get the rewards from it quickly."

That infectious sense of independence is critical to the entrepreneurial spirit. And it's a major reason the spirit of enterprise is increasingly celebrated around the globe, whether in Hong Kong, where free-wheeling entrepreneurship is moving across the border into China's Guangdong and Fujian provinces, or in Germany, where that country's midsize companies—the so-called *Mittelstand*—are a dynamic engine of growth.

Or consider Brazil, where Ricardo Semler, a thirtysomething executive has become the Lee Iacocca of his native country. Semler took over his family's troubled manufacturing company—a rather unglamorous business producing pumps, mixers, and valves—and increased sales more than sixfold, to nearly $30 million, in the past decade. Revenue per employee jumped from $10,800 to $114,000 in the same period.

The story of Semler's efforts to create a model workplace—where employees set their own salaries and have unlimited access to the company's financial records—became the best-selling nonfiction book in Latin American history. "Most companies are still reluctant to bring real democracy into the workplace," Samler contends. "People say they want participative management, but no one wants to delegate the important decisions."

That's a lesson many larger companies, seeking in Jack Welch's words to infuse a "big-company body" with a "small-company soul," are trying hard to learn. They're flattening hierarchies, delegating authority, altering compensation schemes, and empowering workers—all in the hopes of gaining the powerful economies of entrepreneurship. What de Tocqueville would surely notice today is not only the multitude of small enterprising companies but how they—and the spirit that infuses them—are reshaping economies and markets around the world.

By John Byrne

PART 1
Small Is Powerful

1

Just What Is an Entrepreneur?

*It seems to be in the blood, that quality to run
with a dream. Also essential: A love of risk and
a high tolerance for ambiguity.*

Imagine this:

You're a bright young CPA from Cleveland who has decided that the world of Big Eight accounting is simply too rigid to be tolerated. You have a good friend who sells business forms for a living, and before long, you're noticing the large number of invoices, routing slips, and other custom forms your clients use regularly. One day, a light bulb goes on: Your mind transforms the prosaic into a thing of lucrative beauty. Business forms, you decide, hold the key to your wealth and happiness.

So you hang a shingle, buy an answering machine, and start pounding the pavement as an independent business-form rep. You convince General Electric Co. you're for real and get your first big order. Soon, other orders are flowing in, and the business is booming at 40% gross margins. But you're more ambitious than that. You want to run a business, not just sell business forms.

Another idea strikes you, this one more gutsy: Why not sell business-form franchises and expand nationwide? Franchise fees could provide expansion capital, and more outlets would mean volume discounts from manufacturers. You do the homework, set it up, and before long you've got 15 outlets with annual sales of $5 million.

Then, disaster strikes. Out of the blue, your bank gets panicky because you're financing your franchisees' receivables. The asset belongs to the franchise, they say, and can't legally collateralize your $500,000 line of credit. You figure there must be a solution, but one day, the bankers call the loan and turn ugly. "You know," one of them says, "when we foreclose on a company, we padlock the doors and put Doberman pinschers inside so the owner can't even come through the window."

Nice. Gregory P. Muzzillo, the founder and chairman of ProForma Inc., lived through this nightmare. For six months afterward, his days were a constant reminder that he might lose it all. It wasn't himself he was worried about so much as the people who had come to count on him. "It was very frightening," he says, "because other people's lives were depending on my decisions."

Muzzillo found another bank. And ProForma is now a thriving chain with 102 outlets and $30 million in sales. Soon, he will enter a joint venture with Fred DeLuca, the founder of Subway Sandwiches. That means more capital and more expansion. And it means that Greg Muzzillo, after investing just $250 to start, is on his way to becoming a very wealthy man.

Management guru Peter F. Drucker has a theory about entrepreneurs. His notion is that anybody from any organization can learn how to be one. There's nothing mysterious about it, he writes in his book *Innovation and Entrepreneurship*. Those two things are "purposeful tasks that can be organized—are in need of being organized." They are, he writes, "systematic work."

Drucker introduces his book, however, with this disclaimer: He won't be discussing "psychology and character traits." It's an important point. While he's probably right that the nuts and bolts of entrepreneurship can be studied and learned, the soul of an entrepreneur is something else altogether. "An entrepreneur can be a professional manager, and a professional manager can be an entrepreneur," says Gerald R. Blackie, founder of Platinum Software Corp., a fast-growing maker of financial-management programs. "But not every manager can be an entrepreneur."

People who successfully innovate and start businesses come in all shapes and sizes. But they do have a few things others do not. In the deepest sense, they are willing to accept risk for what they believe in. They have the ability to cope with a professional life riddled by ambiguity—a consistent lack of clarity. Most have a drive to put their imprint on whatever they are creating. And while unbridled ego can be a destructive thing, try to find an entrepreneur whose ego isn't wrapped up in the enterprise.

Drucker is right that the task of entrepreneurship has to be organized. The discipline involved in managing growth and innovation is crucial for success. Some people have that skill innately, but most need to learn it. And in an era when entrepreneurs—from Bill Gates to Sam Walton—have become America's heroes, business schools from coast to coast have developed programs to teach the ins and outs of entrepreneurial finance and management.

Business experience from a corporate job is invaluable, too. Ely Callaway, chairman of Callaway Golf Co., spent 17 years at Burlington Industries Inc. before he was snubbed for the CEO's job and stepped out on his own. He ran a winery before launching Callaway Golf, where he hit it big by developing the Big Bertha driver. For all his success as an entrepreneur, Callaway still credits Burlington for honing his business instincts. His attitude: "I'd rather learn how to ride a bike on somebody else's bicycle than on my own."

But learning those skills is about limiting risk, not creating the desire to take the risk. "You can teach people who want to be entrepreneurs that they can think rationally about that career," says Irving H. Grousbeck, a Stanford University business school professor who spent 17 years running a startup called Continental Cablevision Inc. But "can I teach people to be creative and driven?" he asks. "I'm not interested in that." William D. Bygrave, who runs the Center for Entrepreneurial Studies at Babson College, agrees. While he thinks his students are plenty entrepreneurial, he also believes it's a self-limiting population. Those who aren't cut out for it don't tend to show up.

The fact is, entrepreneurs have what author Tom Wolfe called *the right stuff*. And that doesn't mean the macho persona of Chuck Yeager, Wolfe's protagonist. It's another quality Yeager has that, in some measure, is common to most successful entrepreneurs. Yeager's years of experience in the cockpit and his uncanny talent for flying airplanes made his perception of risk different from other people's when it came to testing new designs. He was willing to innovate because he knew he knew how.

Look at Scott Schmidt, the "entrepreneur" who popularized what has become known as extreme skiing. Schmidt jumps from 60-foot cliffs for a living. Ski-equipment companies sponsor him, and people make videos of his jumps. From the chairlift, he appears a reckless maniac. But for every jump, he has carefully charted the takeoff point and landing. And after he leaps, he trusts that his extraordinary talent will help him cope with what comes his way as he falls. His pioneering work has broken the path for an "industry" of extreme skiers—some of whom have been more reckless and died. Schmidt doesn't consider himself reckless. He considers himself a damn good skier.

But comparing entrepreneurs to test pilots and cliff skiers runs the danger of buying into the popular image of entrepreneurs as daredevils. Most of them aren't. "You don't have to be a circus barker," says Grousbeck. "You don't have to be impulsive or flamboyant." You just have to have an idea—and a need to see your idea come out your way. Independence matters most to an entrepreneur (chart). The confidence that flows from ownership of the idea creates the drive to endure the often dire consequences of that independence.

Consider the case of Scott D. Cook, the 40-year-old founder of a hot, $100 million PC software company called Intuit Inc. Cook is no daredevil. "I'm actually pretty conservative by nature," he says. He was no babe in the woods, either, when he launched Intuit.

Cook had grown up the son of an entrepreneur. His father made industrial fire extinguishers, and Scott recalls childhood weekends spent in the garage screwing metal pipes together ("They told me they were for missiles," he says). Before setting out on his own, he spent three years at Procter & Gamble Co. working on the Crisco brand and another three years as a consultant at Bain & Co. Neither really suited him. He liked the work, but not the politics.

His epiphany came one night in 1982 when his wife, Signey Ostby, began complaining about the software program she was using to pay bills. Had she known what she was getting herself into, she would have kept quiet. Cook and Signey's sister began to study the market and discovered a lot of people hated their financial-planning software. The available programs were too complicated. They had too many features customers didn't need.

As far as Cook could tell, financial-planning software was a consumer business. The problem was, it was run by technoids. "The guys out there didn't survey the market," he says. "It was classic P&G: Everybody does it, and everybody has a problem." For Cook, that was rationale enough. As long as he could develop a better product, the risk looked like one worth taking. So he turned to Tom Proulx, a Stanford computer whiz. Then a senior, Proulx banged out a prototype called Quicken. After testing it successfully on accounting neophytes, Cook started calling venture capitalists in late 1983.

He figured credibility would be a problem. He was, after all, a former Crisco salesman teamed with a college student. What bothered the venture capitalists, though, was Quicken itself: Many lamented its dearth of features next to such programs as Home Accountant and Dollars & Sense. Simplicity, Cook argued, was what the customer wanted. The prevailing wisdom in computerdom was that complexity was good. Cook's consumerism was too foreign a concept.

Cook and Proulx plunged ahead anyway. They worked without salaries and rounded up two small investors. Cook added his savings, his Bain profit sharing, his credit cards, and two loans from his parents to create a $400,000 pot of initial capital. They knew they would need more to market Quicken properly, but they figured time was of the essence.

By 1985, however, the money was gone. The last bit was spent on a fruitless ad in *PC* magazine. April 30 brought the blackest moment of Cook's career: He had to tell his six other employees he couldn't pay them. The rest of the year was utter hell. "I was stuck," Cook says. "I knew if I went bankrupt, I'd be paying off the debts for the rest of my life. If someone had walked in and said, 'I'll buy it,' I'd have said, 'Here's the keys.'" As for his personal life, "My wife thought that I had gotten us into a big hole. I still had faith I had the right product, but the thought of losing it all was driving her to distraction. Our marriage came within inches of blowing up."

Cook found a solution in late 1985. He had been trying to convince a number of banks to buy Quicken and resell it to their customers. Finally they came through. Direct mail sales followed and eventually retail distribution. By this March, Cook and Proulx took a booming Intuit public. That was a thrill, but it has left Cook with no illusions about entrepreneurship. He's not even sure how he got through 1985. "I just thought it would be a lot easier than that," he says. "The thrill is there as long as the paycheck is there. But if it's not, the thrill goes away real quick."

Platinum Software's Gerald Blackie knows what Cook has been through. He says entrepreneurs get by with an innate ability to compartmentalize their fears and doubts. Platinum, which has been growing briskly, is a $39 million maker of software to help companies manage finances. But it almost derailed in 1991 when a distribution deal with IBM soured miserably. Facing the threat of bankruptcy "is the worst nightmare you can have," Blackie says. "But you have to put those feelings in a box and close it. If you really analyzed them, you wouldn't do what you have to do."

It is often said that entrepreneurs tend to be blind optimists, but that's too simple a formulation. More likely, they believe in what they're doing with a passion that overcomes doubt—a passion that allows them to contain the feelings Blackie talks about.

William Gorog, founder of the Lexis and Nexis data-base systems, has lately been developing a product designed by his son John. It is a telephone turned interactive transaction device. The Gorogs took a phone, equipped it with special software, and attached a wand that reads bar codes. Wave the wand over a catalog to order groceries, pay bills, conduct bank business—you name it. Gorog formed U.S. Order in 1990 and got an aircraft charter company called World Corp to back him. Sprint, Bell South, and Bell Atlantic have signed on to help sell the devices.

But in the past year, the landscape has changed dramatically. Blaring from every newsstand has been talk of "the information highway" and interactive television. If all goes as predicted, your TV set may soon be able to do everything U.S. Order's ScanFone promises. Gorog's reaction: "I thought, 'Hot damn! People finally understand what we're talking about.'"

Gorog's lieutenants were a little less sanguine. They pondered for a month over how to react. In the end, their solution was brilliant. They decided to sell the phones for the five to seven years it will take to get interactive TV off the ground and see how the market develops from there. Meantime, they will sell to prospective competitors U.S. Order's ability to provide interactive transaction services—expertise those companies would otherwise have to develop on their own. "Our niche is to offer these back-end services to anybody," Gorog says. "This wasn't part of our original strategy. [But] if you don't reexamine what you're doing often, you'll end up out on the limb of a tree." Psychologizing always has its limits, but Paul Shipman, founder of Seattle's booming Red Hook Ale Brewery, is convincing when he speaks of an entrepreneur's "bright side and dark side." The bright side is the ability to strategize and implement effectively. The dark side is the highly personal set of motivations that makes failure intolerable. Shipman latched onto brewing as a way to differentiate himself from a family of lawyers. "It was a very long shadow and a very powerful competitive issue," he says. "It's real primal stuff. Entrepreneurship is primal, right at its root."

Shipman, too, ran out of money when Red Hook's brew lost fizz at the retail level. He reformulated it, pushed ahead, and now has $44 million from a syndicate led by General Electric Capital Corp. to build a new brewery in a Seattle suburb. "In the face of a situation that by all logic is a certified disaster," Shipman says, "the entrepreneur can't countenance defeat."

Many an entrepreneur, of course, finds that the life is not defined by Sturm und Drang. For Mark B. Emmer, who founded tiny Catspaw Inc., owning a company is an excuse to live where he wants (at the heart of the Rockies, in Salida, Colo.) and do what he wants (write software that helps users organize their computers to easily manipulate bodies of text).

While Emmer has been successful selling to academics and publishers, he has had his share of troubles. A deal with Prentice-Hall Inc. to distribute his products fell through when Simon & Schuster Inc. bought the publisher and ordered it out of the software business. Emmer recovered. And he kind of likes that his smallness ($60,000 in sales) lets him keep direct contact with his customers. "The best times are when they say: 'Your program's wonderful. Here's what I'm doing with it.' One guy said we were the secret weapon that let him underbid his competition."

For Emmer, Catspaw is mostly a labor of love. With his wife, Nancy, he has taught himself to advertise, put together direct-mail programs, and buy packaging. In a sense, he has learned for himself what Drucker calls "organizing" the entrepreneurial endeavor. But Emmer also came equipped with the intangibles Drucker doesn't talk about. "From the first, I had no real fear of taking a risk or being out of a job," he says. "I felt I was bright enough that I could support myself and my wife. What other people would see as a risk, I saw as dancing on my toes." Chuck Yeager might put it differently. But you can bet he knows what Emmer is talking about.

By Michael Oneal, with Sandra D. Atchison

2
Meet the
Giant Killers

How do small companies power the economy?
By fostering "creative destruction."

For 150 years, Marxist canon predicted that the first step on the road to the great proletarian revolution would be the destruction of small businesses by their larger competitors. Today, one of communism's last disciples, Cuban President Fidel Castro, has a far different view. He's opening up 100 trades and services—from computer programming to hairdressing—to individual enterprise. Fidel, it seems, is betting that small business can dig him out of the rubble of his island's economy.

In his way, Castro is thrusting Cuba into the middle of one of today's hottest debates: Does small business hold the key to growth? Can an economy develop its full potential without the prodding and innovation of its entrepreneurs?

The issue is white-hot around the globe. In eastern Europe, small businesses are struggling to find their role in emerging capitalist economies. China is grappling with the paradox of freeing its people's entrepreneurial spirit while crushing democracy. Latin American nations are trying to adapt enterprise to their near-feudal economies. And in the U.S., economists argue over how many jobs small businesses create while politicians squabble over whether to give small firms special incentives.

A handful of the hottest entrepreneurial outfits—5% or so—probably do create a big chunk of the jobs in the U.S. At the same time, the bulk of the nation's 6 million small companies live a more modest existence. The majority die within a few years. The bulk of the survivors provide little more than a decent income for their owners and a living wage for a handful of employees.

But quarrels over direct job-creation miss the point. The real value of entrepreneurial companies may be the way they force larger competitors to respond to innovation, from new technology to new markets. That process, which Austrian economist Joseph Schumpeter aptly dubbed "creative destruction," is not pretty, but it may be necessary for a thriving capitalist system. "Creating jobs is a pillar of a modern economy," says Zoltan Acs, an economist at the University of Baltimore. "But the other pillar is the role of innovation and technological change. Small firms have become a driving force in that change."

In the U.S., the role of small businesses has waxed and waned. In the earliest days, entrepreneurs launched an industrial revolution. Eli Whitney helped lay the groundwork for mass production by developing early machine tools and designing a way to produce guns from interchangeable parts. By the dawn of the 20th century, the trusts dominated the U.S. economy. But entrepreneurs still drove innovation. Consider George Westinghouse, who remade the industrial world by promoting alternating-current electricity, despite opposition from most of the business Establishment.

The U.S. economy is now in the midst of another dramatic transition. From World War II to the early 1980s, the credo was: "Bigger is better." Economists from Adam Smith to Karl Marx had trumpeted the power of size. Managers strove for economies of scale—whether they were building nuclear power plants or corporate conglomerates. Small companies just didn't matter.

In some capital-intensive industries, such as telecommunications and aircraft manufacturing, size may still be important. But for much of the economy, the conventional wisdom no longer holds. The leveraged buyouts of the 1980s went a long way toward busting up many of the biggest conglomerates. New technology enabled startups to bypass the 60-year-old industrial processes burdening older rivals. Global competition exposed the weakness of many industrial giants.

Small companies are hardly immune to business cycles. In the past few years, thousands of them succumbed to the credit crunch and a sharp decline in consumption. But while big companies are still struggling with painful downsizing, more resilient smaller outfits are riding dramatic long-term trends.

Today, bulk seems to be losing out to agility and speed. "There is a tremendous gap in the speed of product development," says Larry Prusak, a specialist in business communications at Ernst & Young. "In big firms, you have to get a business plan, then you have to do a budget. But if you have 50 people, you can order 10 pizzas, figure out what you have to do, and come back in two weeks with a decision."

Sam Walton, a five-and-dime manager from Arkansas, changed the very nature of retailing. Big steel was chased from the structural steel business by a horde of domestic minimills. "The basic structure of our economy is undergoing constant change," says Bruce Kirchoff, professor of entrepreneurship at New Jersey Institute of Technology. "And it's initiated by new business formation and growth."

That dynamism has spawned a virtual cult of the entrepreneur. Bookstores are awash with titles on how to start a business. Corporate refugees are thinking small. Big companies are scrambling to remake themselves in the image of the entrepreneur. And college kids, who may once have aspired to life in the corner office, now have other goals. Says small-business consultant David Birch: "There is a whole world of 24-year-olds who never dreamed of going to work for a big company."

Nowhere is the revolutionary potential of entrepreneurship more evident than in steel. In 1960, the industry was dominated by a handful of big producers. Minimills—small outfits that make steel by melting scrap in electric furnaces—had a puny 2% market share. Today they account for nearly one-third of finished steel shipments.

Aggressive companies such as Nucor Corp. did not invent the minimill, but they married technology to marketing skill and management innovations such as performance-based pay. Today, many are more productive than either integrated U.S. companies or foreign mills.

Minimills broke the monopoly of Big Steel. And they may have saved the U.S. steel industry. Says Christopher Plummer, director of steel analysis at Resources Strategies Inc.: "Technological change driven by minimills has been the primary factor of change in the steel industry."

And there may be still more innovations from a new generation of upstarts. In recent years, Nucor has had great success making high-quality flat rolled steel at its plant in Crawfordsville, Ind. In August, plant manager Keith Busse left the company to form a startup minimill of his own. "Nucor is pretty darn awfully efficient," says Busse. But "you might improve it 10%. There are new forms of technology which haven't been employed by Nucor."

Entrepreneurs can overhaul an existing industry or build a new one. Back in the early 1980s, a few upstarts such as Apple Computer Inc. and Osborne Computer Co. believed they could put a PC in every home and office in America. At the time, they were ridiculed by the mainframe makers who dominated the industry.

And what of those behemoths today? Most have been supplanted by outfits that didn't even exist a decade ago. In 1982, Michael Dell was in high school, and only the nerdiest gearhead would think of buying a computer through the mail. Today, Dell Computer Corp. alone is selling $2 billion worth of mail-order hardware and has more than 4,000 employees. With its low overhead, Dell could offer bargain prices. But it also offered good service, which many other mail-order operations lacked. More important, dozens of companies like Dell's have made PCs virtual commodities, available to nearly everyone who wants them. That alone has profoundly changed the U.S. economy.

Computer software has followed almost the same script. In 1980, most of the biggest software producers were mainframe outfits, names from the dim past such as Burroughs and NCR. Since then, the software business has exploded. But the old guard has been left behind by newcomers such as Novell Inc. and Computer Associates International, Inc. How rapid has change been? Well, in 1980, Microsoft had all of 125 employees. Today it can boast 12,000. "The whole computer business has been turned upside down," says Kirchoff, "and it's been because of innovations brought into the marketplace by new small firms."

High tech gets all the glamour, but enterprise also is changing much more mundane industries. Small lumber mills, for instance, are developing a powerful presence in exports, a market largely ignored by bigger companies. "There are phenomenal success stories," says University of Washington economist Anne Illinitch. "You drive into the backwoods of nowhere, and there are companies doing 100% of their business with Germany or Spain."

Even in banking, where established institutions are feverishly merging their way into new markets, entrepreneurs continue to find important niches. Consider Steven Kaplan of Woodbridge, N.J., who fills the role of the old-time local banker for restaurants, lending money, providing advice, and making connections with suppliers. After being laid off from a management job at CBS in 1986, he went to work for Transmedia Inc., one of Business Week's hot-growth companies over the past two years. In 1990, Kaplan bought the company's first franchise.

Many banks avoid restaurants as too risky, but Kaplan has found them to be a lucrative niche. In 1990, he lent about $100,000 to 40 restaurants in New Jersey. This year, he'll lend more than $2 million to more than 150 establishments, using a system that allows restaurants to pay off their loans with food and beverage credits. Transmedia then resells these meals at a discount to consumers, who purchase a Transmedia restaurant card. Kaplan, who has only one salesperson, won't show up in government statistics as a big job-creator, but he, along with Transmedia franchisees in 14 other states, provides financing for thousands of other small businesses.

How do the upstarts do it? In part, it's because the big, bureaucratic dinosaurs are slow to adapt to change. "The success of small business reflects the failure of big companies," says Richard Florida, director of the Center for Economic Development at Carnegie Mellon University.

At the same time, entrepreneurs have some powerful economic trends in their favor. The labor force is highly mobile. Capital is available, although more often from Uncle Harry than from a bank. PCs and faxes have sharply reduced the cost of entry—an individual can start a small service business for under $20,000. Consumer demand for well-made, specialized products has reduced the advantages of big, assembly-line factories. Add to all that one big cultural factor—in the U.S., as in few other nations, risk is a virtue and failure can be overcome. "If you fail in the U.S.," says Florida, "you have the opportunity to try again."

But why do some startups make it while others flop? Paul Reynolds, professor of entrepreneurial studies at Marquette University, looked at 1,400 new companies in Pennsylvania and Minnesota and found 27 "high performers" that grew at an average annual rate of 150% for at least five years.

His study confirms some suspicions—and explodes a few myths. One key finding: Small business creates lots of jobs, all right, but most of them in just a handful of companies. Reynolds found that the most successful were in manufacturing and wholesale trade. Only one was in high tech. While use of technology and price were important to the fortunes of the best new companies, quality of goods and services was even more critical. And he found that the most successful startups were formed by teams—often refugees from established companies—who focused on financial controls.

Reynolds couldn't find many tinkers who built better mousetraps in their garages. Instead, he paints a picture of veteran entrepreneurs who grab an opportunity and run with it. "The major distinction is time," he says. "These hypergrowth firms put their businesses together faster than anybody else."

Perhaps the biggest threat to that kind of aggressive entrepreneur comes from another recent trend in the U.S. economy—the move toward outsourcing. Many big companies such as General Electric Co. and DuPont Co. recently have been forming extremely close relationships with small suppliers.

Those Japanese-like arrangements generate a steady source of income for the small firms and improve productivity. But they may also drain the smaller partners of the entrepreneurial spirit that made them successful in the first place.

Yet the entrepreneur of legend remains a powerful force. In a separate study, Reynolds found that at any given time, 4% of the adult population of Wisconsin is trying to start a small business, 80% of them while working full-time at another job. Why not dream the dreams of George Eastman, who invented his Kodak camera in his off hours while working as a Rochester (N.Y.) bank clerk? Or of Jack Daniel, who at 14 bought a still from his boss—the local distiller and Lutheran minister. Daniel not only made good whiskey but also realized the importance of moving to the railroad town of Lynchburg, Tenn., where he could ship throughout the South. By the turn of the century, Daniel had built a national market for what had traditionally been a local product.

Increasingly, hitting the entrepreneurial jackpot is a vision for people around the world. But will small business drive reform in newly capitalist countries? John E. Jackson, a professor of business administration at the University of Michigan, thinks it could.

Jackson looked at Michigan businesses from 1978 too 1988, a period of great transition in the state. Michigan lost a staggering 200,000 auto manufacturing jobs but saw a boomlet in nonauto manufacturing and services. Jackson found that in 1978, 55% of all manufacturing jobs were in companies with more than 500 employees. He estimates that share today is less than 40%. "The resurgence of small business is a key factor in the resurgence of the Michigan economy," Jackson says.

These days, Jackson is doing his research in Poland, and he sees some surprising similarities. There, old state factories are having a terrible time raising capital, while small companies—retailers, business services, and factories—are showing real vibrancy.

No doubt Eastern Europe is fascinated by Western-style small business. But there are real differences between U.S. startups and their Western European or Japanese counterparts. Small Japanese companies seem to be thriving, but most serve as little more than suppliers to dominant big companies. In Italy and France, small outfits are also doing fine, supported by heavy state subsidies. But something seems to be missing: the entrepreneurial innovation that defines the best of the U.S. small companies. Could a Microsoft in Paris challenge Groupe Bull? Not likely.

It might have a better chance in Hong Kong, where freewheeling entrepreneurs are a dynamic force for change. Germany seems to have found a middle ground. There, 300,000 small and midsize companies generate a big chunk of the nation's export growth. Some see them as a model for small business in Eastern Europe.

There seems little doubt that entrepreneurs will play a key role in the world's emerging economies. But will they follow the heavily subsidized yet less innovative French model? Or will they try to copy the U.S.? And entrepreneurs in the U.S. have some questions of their own to answer. Should they push for special tax breaks, along with government technical and financial assistance? Or are they better off left alone? After all, the keys to success for U.S. entrepreneurs seem to lie more with free-flowing capital and flexible labor markets rather than state subsidies.

Consultant Birch has called the best of these dynamic companies "gazelles." But he may have picked the wrong animal. The critical role of entrepreneurs may be more akin to wolves: aggressive and skilled at culling out the old and sick. That's the creative destruction that Schumpeter talked about, and it may be the real story of how the best small companies drive change in a healthy economy.

By Howard Gleckman, with Stephen Baker and Jonathan B. Levine

PART 2

The New Economies of Scale

3

Technology— Start with Some High-Tech Magic

Used wisely, technology can make companies fast and flexible.

It's early August on Canada's Cape Breton Island. Bald eagles wheel overhead as Terrence B. Magrath and Katherine Busboom Magrath sail their yawl along the rocky shores of the island's Bras d'Or Lake. The isolation is magnificent. But take a closer look. What's that brightly colored screen? It's connected to a 486-class personal computer below deck. The Magraths are using it to plot a new course—not for the yawl, but for the $500 million in investments they manage.

Wall Street is just a keystroke away. When the Magraths' calculations are complete, they're sent on radio waves to a cellular-phone antenna on the island. In a matter of seconds, they reach the couple's home in Marblehead, Mass., where associates place orders with traders on the New York Stock Exchange and elsewhere. Over four days, in between spells of eagle watching, the pair overhaul the holdings managed by their firm, ValueQuest Ltd., whose big-name clients range from 3M to the California Public Employee Retirement System.

A few years ago, a 12-person firm like ValueQuest couldn't have taken on such giants of money management as Fidelity and Putnam—from a boat, no less. What keeps it in the game is what might be called the technology of small. It includes PCs, cellular phones, and Lotus Development Corp.'s Notes—software that organizes the flow of work. In the 1970s, at Terry Magrath's last employer, it required 20 people to manage back-office bookkeeping. Today, he says, "we do it with 1½ people, and we do it better."

If technology is letting small companies act big, it's doing something else as well: It lets big companies act small—to be quick and flexible, and to know their customers as intimately as corner merchants know theirs.

Look at what this has done for Consolidated Rail Corp. Until recently, the Eastern freight line was a Gulliver being bedeviled by trucks. Conrail was tied down by rigid union work rules, outdated regulations, and a 1960s system for handling documents. Conductors would sit in the caboose thumbing through papers, trying to tell whether their train was running with the right cars. Moreover, because trains didn't move until they had a full complement of cars, delivery times were unreliable—so much so that some customers employed people to figure out where the railroad had their cargo.

Now, the paper "waybills" for each car have been replaced by electronic messages, improving reliability and speed. On top of that, Conrail keeps to a schedule instead of waiting until it has a full string of cars. The cost of doing that now and then is offset by savings from increased predictability: Conrail pays fewer away-from-home penalties to crews, for example. To be more responsive to its customers, meanwhile, the railroad has divided itself into four networks for different kinds of cargo, from cars to commodities. Says Ralph von dem Hagen, vice-president for customer services: "It's a big business, but we're sort of operating like a small one."

Some small business—with 12,400 route miles in 13 states and Canada. The point, of course, is that technology is transformative. It can amplify the powers of small companies or help big companies bust their bureaucracies. By sharing computer networks, companies or their divisions can concentrate on what they do best and can farm out the rest to partners. Jessica

Lipnack and Jeffrey Stamps, co-authors of *The TeamNet Factor*, have spotted such networks everywhere from Denmark to northern Italy to Minnesota.

In short, the technology of small is remaking the economy. It's helping big companies compete internationally, while helping smaller ones grow faster. So far, the effect is most pronounced in the white-collar world. But even in factories, traditional notions of economies of scale are changing. Big companies are embracing technology that lets them emulate more flexible job shops. And far-sighted small manufacturers are buying the precision machinery needed to compete with, or at least to supply, multinational giants.

To be sure, the gadgetry has to be used wisely. General Motors Corp. could have bought Toyota Motor Corp. three times over with what it put into capital spending in the 1980s, yet it lost market share. A chastened General Electric Co. has ripped out some factory automation, including at a helicopter-engine-parts line in Lynn, Mass. last year. Says Gary M. Reiner, vice-president for business development: "We have found that technology in many instances impedes productivity"—if it reduces flexibility.

Indeed, big companies' problems with technology often stem from sclerosis. Two years ago, Raymond L. Manganelli's New York consulting firm, Gateway Information Services Inc., was helping a client weed out useless computer reports. He found one that was being churned out regularly for an employee who had died in 1958: "He had asked for that report very, very early on in the history of automation, and it was included in each upgrading or rebuilding of the system," says Manganelli.

Small businesses, by contrast, are more likely to underuse than overuse the new tools. The owners may be too busy, too short on cash—or just too set in their ways—to invest even in gear that would quickly pay for itself. That's a chronic problem for small manufacturers. "Most of them are far behind," says Leo Reddy, president of Washington's National Coalition for Advanced Manufacturing. No wonder that, according to the Industrial Technology Institute in Ann Arbor, Mich., the productivity of big manufacturers exceeds that of small ones—and the gap has been widening ever since recordkeeping began in 1958.

The good news is that a younger generation of small-business people—those who are in their 20s, 30s, and 40s—is eagerly embracing the new machines and software. Take J. Bronce Henderson III, 42. In 1980, he joined his father's $2 million-a-year job shop, Detroit Center Tool. Soon, he spotted enormous opportunities. Rivals were sticking loyally—and foolishly, he thought—to outmoded production gear. "It's easy to fall in love with 30-year-old equipment that has zero book value and figure you have a low cost of production," Henderson says.

Instead of counting pennies, Henderson bought new gear and moved up to making welding and assembly robots for the auto industry. Today, DCT Cos. does $150 million a year in revenue and counts Toyota, Nissan, and Honda as customers. "I'm a technology junkie," Henderson says. "I can't always explain it to my accountant. But at the end of the day, with new equipment, I have better quality, higher productivity, and our costs are lower."

Another tech junkie, 34-year-old Andrew W. Harris, resigned from Apple Computer Inc. in 1991—disappointed, he says, that the company wasn't encouraging its employees to work from home. He thought this would save money and unleash creativity. In 1989, while still at Apple, he co-founded San Francisco-based Telemorphix Inc., a company with no headquarters. Its 30 employees, most of whom create interactive television programs, work mainly at home and keep in touch by phone, fax, and computer. PacerForum, a program from Pacer Software that's akin to Lotus Notes, serves as their virtual office space. Says Harris: "This liberates us. If we find someone extremely talented who's in London, they don't have to move."

There are lots of other guerilla entrepreneurs. At age 8, Kelly J. Loneman began playing with a Commodore computer. At 20, he tried to persuade silkscreen companies in Omaha to throw away their pens and prepare clothing designs on Macintoshes. They didn't—so Loneman did, making designs with a borrowed Mac in his parents' basement. At 24, he owns an Omaha company, Koala Tee Custom Sportswear Inc., with sales of $1 million a year. Using the Mac, he can deliver a shirt in one week instead of two.

Like other techno-savvy entrepreneurs, Loneman latches on anything that might give him an edge. He signed up for a phone-company data service called Integrated Services Digital

Network after reading about it in a local business journal. It has let him centralize production in an old industrial section of town, where his plant should be able to receive computerized orders in only 20 seconds from storefronts around the country. Loneman has one shop in West Omaha and is planning another in Kansas City, Mo., next year. "We can go into another city or area of town with just two people," he adds.

Can a giant company emulate the entrepreneurial spirit of Terry and Katherine Magrath, Andy Harris, or Kelly Loneman? Probably not, if it's organized hierarchically. In those cases, the main function of middle management is to pass information up from the bottom and orders down from the top. "Eighty percent of what companies do these days is controls or hand-offs," says consultant Manganelli.

Lands' End Inc. in Dodgeville, Wis., is trying to eliminate many of those controls and hand-offs through computer networking. Items in the catalog of the $700 million mail-order clothing company tend to run out. To avoid that, an inventory manager has to notice that the stocks are getting low, then call a salesperson for the manufacturer, who tells the factory's production planner. With vacations and telephone tag slowing things down, "Lord knows, weeks could go by," says Gary R. Steuck, vice-president for inventory management.

But on 15% of items, the ordering loop has been drastically shortened. For those, Lands' End inventory reports go directly to the factory by computer hookup. With faster feedback, production is better calibrated and "stock-outs" are far rarer. Some suppliers' salespeople resisted the change, fearing that they would lose influence by being cut out of the loop. But Steuck says they now like it, too. Freed from the drudgery of processing reorders, they can work on persuading Lands' End to include their clothes in future catalogs. Steuck says he hopes to get 85% of items on the system in two to three years.

Big companies that act small also do it by using technology as a servant of their individual business units. Merrill Lynch & Co. adopted that philosophy three years ago, after DuWayne Peterson Jr., a technical whiz, was succeeded as chief information officer by Edward L. Goldberg, who had more experience in management. Under Peterson, the programmers had been all in one place. Units such as retail brokerages had to wait in line for software requests. Goldberg gave each unit its own programmers, increasing responsiveness without increasing staff. Says Howard P. Sorgen, senior vice-president for global information services: "In the way we employ technologies, we are an amalgam of small businesses."

Skeptics question whether makeovers such as Merrill Lynch's really are motivated by advances in computers and other technical gear. The real impetus, they say, is management philosophy. "Technology is almost entirely an enabler and very rarely a driver of change," argues Gary W. Loveman, assistant professor at Harvard business school.

You don't have to agree with Loveman 100% to think of cases where the best solution is low-tech. Sharam Shirazi, a Silicon Valley executive, recalls how a previous employer, chipmaker Zilog Inc., overcame internecine warfare. "Everyone in Building C [marketing] and Building D [engineering] hated each other. So we meshed them in one place. They ended up liking each other," says Shirazi.

Detroit calls that "co-location." Chrysler Corp. used it to solidify the teams of researchers, designers, manufacturing experts, and marketers who created its LH sedan and new Neon subcompact. Says Shirazi, now marketing vice-president in Menlo Park, Calif., for Teknekron Corp., a diversified electronics and software company: "E-mail, speaker-phones—those are for conveying information. If I really need someone's help, nothing beats going over to him and saying: 'John, I need your help. Let's sit down.'"

But what if John is 2,000 miles away? In such cases, the answer may be ad hoc, fluid arrangements—the virtual corporation—and that's where information systems come to the fore. For a glimpse of one possible future, visit Bruce L. Egan, a consultant for phone companies who works from Jackson Hole, Wyo. Since he moved from Manhattan two years ago, Egan says, "my productivity is up, not down. The reason is that the daily ridiculousness doesn't happen."

Consultants like Egan have operated from garden spots for years. One difference now is the size of the jobs with which they're entrusted—in his case, contracts of up to $500,000 for helping phone companies plan and market new services. He and his far-flung collaborators aren't taking crumbs of work from giants such as Arthur Andersen, Marsh & McClennan, or McGraw-Hill Inc.'s DRI. Quite the contrary: Often, Egan hands off work such as data collection to his larger rivals.

Some customers don't realize how small Egan's operation is, and those who do are able to take it in stride. Egan attributes that to their growing comfort with the networked age. He still prefers having face-to-face meetings for cooking up new ideas. But he adds: "I've worked for a lot of people I've never seen. People just accept that we will take on a large project and complete it satisfactorily."

Harvard's Loveman may be right—that technology is only an enabler of new forms of business organization, not a driver of change. But acolytes of the information age aren't particularly interested in such distinctions. They've proved that the smart application of the new tools can spell success for big companies and small. On this particular golden afternoon, Bruce Egan has a different kind of driver in mind—the kind he's about to use off the first tee.

By Peter Loy, with Tim Smart

4

Management—
Belt-Tightening
the Smart Way

*After savage cutbacks in management, many
large companies are learning to be more
productive with less.*

From Armonk, N.Y., to Zurich, Switzerland, business is on a
weight-loss binge. Over the past five years, even such domi-
neering presences as IBM and ABB Asea Brown Boveri have
shed employees, layers of management, and old ways of doing
things. They have reengineered work processes and raised efficiency by creating quality initiatives, multidisciplinary teams of
workers, and employee empowerment programs. Strip away the
business babble, and it comes down to this: Top-heavy organizations are out. Slender, nimble ones are in. "We need to cultivate
a visceral hatred of bureaucracy," General Electric Co. Chairman
John F. Welch Jr. told his shareholders last year.

Talk all you want about the turbocharging effect on business of
computers, faxes, cellular phones, and high-speed data communications. None of it makes much difference unless it's accompa-
nied by what is coming to be called lean management. Defined
simply, that means eliminating useless work and the people who

do it, and running what's left according to a new set of principles and skills. With entire layers of management gone, senior executives who once ruled by pushing buttons have to learn "team managing, giving and receiving feedback, and diagnosing problems," says Noel M. Tichy, a management professor at the University of Michigan. "Yet this soft stuff is a bunch of crap if it's not combined with hard-nosed performance standards."

Entrepreneurs long ago learned all this by necessity. Undercapitalized and poorly staffed, they had to stretch resources to the limit. For those who survived, that disadvantage became a competitive inspiration: You waste less money and time if you have little of both. Slowly, even Corporate America is seeing that less in the way of resources and management can translate into something good: productivity. "Most struggling companies are overmanaged and underled," believes Lawrence A. Bossidy, chairman of AlliedSignal Inc. "Having too many resources is the basis of a lot of failure. I try to make sure my people don't have enough of what they want."

His logic: Back when large corporations had nearly unlimited budgets, managers spent money indiscriminately. Doling out fewer resources forces these people to focus more on what's best for a business. That's why so many startups, with less capital and smaller research and development budgets, often outpace bigger competitors in bringing out products. "It's a mind-set," Bossidy adds, "more than it is about money."

For many corporations, this amounts to an extraordinary change in attitude. Through the postwar boom, most U.S. industries added staff by the tens of thousands, while piling on rigid controls to help manage the horde of new hires. Revenues and productivity were growing, and companies could afford the extra layers. Beyond that, management convinced itself that large numbers of white-collar staffers were needed to keep up with growth.

That view began to change by the early 1980s, with the onset of global competition. In short order, many companies found their cost structures out of sync with the marketplace. Cutbacks in middle management followed, and with those came another surprise: The managers who remained had to give up a good measure of control to workers. "Ten years ago, we thought that if you had four employees reporting to every manager, your managers were overworked," says Bossidy. "We've discovered that if you have nine, you have less time to manage"—and must rely on subordinates to help out.

This trend may be gathering steam. Consultants and academics say that "spans of control"—the number of employees each manager supervises—have risen to as high as 30 to 1 in divisions of companies such as Ameritech, the Baby Bell. That's largely because people who did much of the staff work—financial analysts, assistant managers, and their like—have disappeared at a staggering rate. "You've got to push out the old work, which was about monitoring, inspecting, and overmanaging," says John W. Humphrey, chief executive of Forum Corp., a Boston consulting and training firm. Unlike some consultants, Humphrey has taken his own advice. Forum, with $40 million in revenues, has eliminated three of its eight levels of management. Some 14 people report to Humphrey vs. five as recently as two years ago, and other Forum executives now manage up to 22 people.

"Five or six years ago, we had a name for that," says Humphrey. "We called it bad management. But if you organize your company for it, it's doable." When one of his subordinates recently hired a No. 2 from outside, he alone made the decision. "Before, he would not have made the offer without my approval."

Going from the old way to the new involves culture shock. People are eliminated, but work isn't, at least not at first. That was true at General Electric, which employed about 400,000 people in the early 1980s and now has about 230,000, even though its revenues have risen 150% in the interim. "Initially at GE, middle managers were dying," says the University of Michigan's Tichy. "The middle managers were saying things like, 'I know adding head-count isn't the answer, but I'm working seven days a week trying to do all the old things, and it isn't working.'" As a consultant at GE during that transition, Tichy helped Welch redesign education and training efforts to make them a critical part of the corporation's transformation.

The turmoil eased once GE eliminated unnecessary tasks, a goal accomplished largely through numerous sessions between managers at all levels who sought to break down GE's bureaucracy. In the company's medical systems group, for example, it

How Lean Is Your Company?

It's hard to find a major corporation that hasn't downsized in recent years. But simple reductions in staffing don't make for lean management. Here's a checklist, developed from interviews with executives and consultants, that may tell you if your company needs a diet.

Company characteristic	Analysis
1. Layers of management between CEO and the shop floor	Some companies, such as Ameritech, now have as few as four or five where as many as 12 had been common. More than six is most likely too many.
2. Number of employees managed by the typical executive	At lean companies, spans of control range up to one manager to 30 staffers. A ratio of lower than 1:10 is a warning of arterial sclerosis.
3. Amount of work cut out by your downsizing	Eliminating jobs without cutting out work can bring disaster. A downsizing should be accompanied by at least a 25% reduction in the number of tasks performed. Some lean companies have hit 50%.
4. Skill levels of the surviving management group	Managers must learn to accept more responsibility and to eliminate unneeded work. Have you taught them how?
5. Size of your largest profit center by number of employees	Break down large operating units into smaller profit centers—less than 500 employees is a popular cutoff—to gain the economies of entrepreneurship and offset the burdens of scale.
6. Post-downsizing size of staff at corporate headquarters	The largest layoffs, on a percentage basis, should be at corporate headquarters. It is often the most overstaffed—and the most removed from customers.

once took eight signatures to get a replacement part for a magnetic resonance imaging system into a hospital. Those approvals had been added over the years for internal, bureaucratic reasons that had long since become obscure—so they were easy to dump. "Now you don't need any," says Tichy, and parts get delivered on demand. "You do what's right for the customer," he adds.

DuPont Co. is another case in point. Like many large companies, the chemical giant began to see vast changes in its markets in the mid-1980s that undermined its economies of scale. In its worldwide nylon business, a $500 million operation, competitors with lower labor costs and similar technology flooded the market and created vast overcapacity. "It put immense pressure on our customers and us," says Robert M. Axtell, worldwide director for DuPont's nylon business.

DuPont's solution was to reduce overhead and make tough choices about what kind of organization it needed to compete. Over a two-year period, Axtell cut 20% to 25% of the staffers in every function, from research to marketing, without significantly affecting the performance of those departments. Two layers of management were stripped out. A unit that had been divided into two segments—the commodity and specialty nylon businesses—was broken into nine. That forced a tighter focus on each business—and gave profit-and-loss responsibility to more managers.

As at GE, the next step was eliminating tasks. In deciding what work to cut, Axtell kept asking: Is it really tied to the bottom line? Does it add value? "A lot of management was just checking the checkers," he says. "There were people around just asking questions and not getting any job done." Since those days, "we have taken the business from a point where it was questionable whether the corporation would invest in us to the point where it will." DuPont does not break out profits for its nylon group.

If getting leaner has taught Axtell a lesson, it's this: Stay in close touch with both your employees and your customers. "You can't communicate enough, because there is a lot of confusion when you restructure," he adds. Move quickly to get it over with, he suggests, and make sure you have time to "do healing" with the survivors. "You must spend a lot of time team-building with the people who are left."

Lean management isn't always about cutting overhead. Sometimes it means placing more emphasis on the company's core work—satisfying customers. Take Pepsi-Cola Co., the huge unit of PepsiCo Inc. In recent years, smaller companies, such as Snapple Beverage Corp., began to chip away at the beverage market dominated by Pepsi and Coca-Cola with fruit drinks, iced tea, and iced coffee. CEO Craig Weatherup says Pepsi found itself "doing things the same old way because that's the way we did things. We had allowed a culture to develop around the notion that we could make [Pepsi], send it down the chute, and take in the money."

Rising competition meant it was no longer that simple. To respond better to retailers, Weatherup streamlined Pepsi last December, cutting the layers of management between himself and customer reps from six to four. He also turned the organization chart on its head, putting the field reps on top. "The right-side-up company," as Weatherup calls Pepsi, "changed from an organization that was focused on satisfying top management to one now focused on the customer."

How so? Before, "when senior management went out to the field, employees were mainly worried about their presentations to us," says Brenda Barnes, chief operating officer. "Now, the focus is on how I can help them make their job easier." Fewer layers of management, she adds, means "you have to empower people." For example, field reps now plot marketing and promotion with customers—without having to get higher approval. Reps who find a product out of stock call for the item immediately instead of waiting days for a normal delivery. The bottom line: Pepsi Cola's U.S. operating earnings in 1993's first half jumped 15%, to $431 million, on a 5% rise in revenues to $2.6 billion.

How do you know if all the fat is gone? "You should never be satisfied that you're lean enough," contends Ernest I. Glickman, managing partner of Harbridge House Inc., a consulting firm. "The best companies will constantly look for ways to slim down." This is one diet, in short, that may never end.

By John Byrne, with Tim Smart

5

Marketing— How to Get Closer to Your Customers

Often, you don't need huge budgets for effective marketing.

They were two of marketing's greatest entrepreneurs. In 1916, Clarence Saunders of Memphis opened a small grocery store— the forerunner of today's Piggly Wiggly—where shoppers, not clerks, picked up items themselves and took them to the cash register. In 1930, Michael Cullen of Long Island added a twist: He turned a parking garage into a spacious supermarket that offered unprecedented variety. To spur demand, Cullen took out big newspaper advertisements to promote name brands such as Ivory soap and Maxwell House coffee. The mass-marketing revolution in America was born—and retailers and brand-name manufacturers were to profit immensely.

Skip forward six decades. Retailers of every stripe are under intense pressure. Merchants and developers have doubled the amount of store space in the U.S. over the past 12 years, even as Americans' real income has barely grown. Giant chains such as Wal-Mart Stores Inc. dominate this glutted market and push their own store brands. Increasingly, established marketers such as Procter & Gamble Co. and Philip Morris Cos. vie for customers who have often concluded that the only difference between brands is price. Private-label and discount cigarettes, for example, now account for 37% of industry sales, up from almost zero 12 years ago.

If classic mass-marketing no longer packs the same punch, what's a company to do? Marketers are starting to answer that question the way Karl A. Steigerwald does: "We have to go back to being small shopkeepers," says the marketing director of Spiegel Inc. Steigerwald obviously doesn't mean tearing down supermarkets. In some ways, the task is more daunting than that: Steigerwald thinks marketers should travel the painful road back to developing relationships with customers who are now grossly overloaded with product choices.

That means thinking small and acting entrepreneurial— whether you're a giant such as Spiegel, PepsiCo, or 3M, or an up-and-comer such as Manco, a duct-tape maker, or Health Valley Foods, a New Age food marketer. It also means stepping back from the old tactics of 30-second commercials, product line extensions, and massive promotions, and thinking instead of new ways to appeal to consumers. Companies both big and small can accomplish this through technology that uses vast new data bases to plumb people's buying habits. Or they may devise promotional strategies that make a marketing campaign especially memorable—and create a tighter bond with the consumer. The idea, whether big or small, is to recapture the drive and originality of Saunders and Cullen.

If those marketers were alive today, they might already have latched onto data-base marketing. That's what Pizza Hut, PepsiCo Inc.'s $3.6 billion fast-food unit, has been doing. This year it is spending an estimated $20 million on this strategy, which involves creating electronic profiles of some 9 million customers who have gotten deliveries of its pizza. Built from phone orders since the company began home delivery in 1984, the data base can track pizza-gobbling habits across the country.

As a result, says marketing chief Robert Perkins, "you can target the relevant message to the right consumer." As a direct marketer for the Republican Party in the 1980s, he pioneered database methods that reaped millions in contributions. Now, his goal at Pizza Hut is "returning marketing to the 19th century," a time when merchants knew their customers by name.

He can't do that exactly. But in promotions this summer, his office sent out coupons that matched the tastes of the addressees: Lovers of Neapolitan-style pizza got offers for those, not for thick-crust pizza. Consumers who had been willing to try new foods got a mailing for Bigfoot, a giant-pizza innovation. Customers who had not ordered in a while got deeper discounts than others. Very precise—and very successful: Analysts expect third-quarter Pizza Hut earnings to rise 25%.

At Spiegel, Karl Steigerwald is thinking 19th century, too. In fact, catalog-merchandise buyers at the $2.2 billion marketer are now nicknamed "shopkeepers." That title reflects the changes Spiegel made in order to rebuild its earnings, which declined 77% between 1989 and 1991. Spiegel executives decided that the company's big catalog had to act like a small, customer-friendly one. To achieve that, Steigerwald told buyers for his book to assume they were creating their own specialty catalogs. Their offerings would then be displayed more distinctly inside the old catalog, somewhat like boutiques in a mall.

Liberated, the buyers surveyed customers to devise "shops" for women who wanted romantic apparel, or for customers who wanted cheaper prices. They also set up a system to track sales by item to make sure the new catalogs-inside-the-catalog reached their intended customers. The result: some 20 catalogs folded inside the big book, and a 12% sales gain in 1992, as well as a 32% jump in operating income.

Spiegel and Pizza Hut are both giants that have used their ample finances to get closer to customers. But small marketers need not despair. They can use sophisticated technology too. And they can use nimbler marketing strategies to outwit bigger rivals.

Jack Kahl knows about taking on giants. The chief executive of Manco Inc. in Westlake, Ohio, has transformed his maker of duct tape and packaging from a $4 million company in 1977 to an $85 million enterprise this year. In giant chains such as Wal-

Mart and Kmart, Manco now leads the market for tape with about a 40% share, up from almost zero in 1979.

His secret: Ignore the conventional wisdom, which says you can't do much with a ho-hum commodity product, especially when you're facing big, well-entrenched competitors. Kahl noticed that customers often called duct tape "duck tape." Why not create a duck mascot and inject some humor in the marketing? "I said: 'If I can make this work, we'll have a brand name,'" recalls Kahl. Soon, a goofy yellow duck was festooning Manco's packaging and in-store displays. Consumer recognition—and sales—took off.

Manco would probably be just a flash in the pan, though, if Kahl had not followed the fun and games with serious legwork. He courted Wal-Mart, offering special computer-based inventory control that dramatically raises efficiency. He also competes with 3M and others on price, cutting costs to retailers by up to 20%. Lacking funds for massive ad campaigns, Kahl sends out 32,000 greeting cards four times a year to buyers and managers at stores he supplies. Retailers also get his newsletter, which prints insights from everyone from Socrates to Thomas Edison. The store managers clearly remember him—and back his products against mighty competitors.

Kahl created a new identity for a tired product. Likewise, W. L. Gore & Associates, the maker of Gore-Tex fabrics, created a new product in a tired category, dental floss. Then, instead of advertising massively, Gore used niche marketing and data-base technology to create customer enthusiasm.

The company's technicians applied their lessons in creating strong fibers to make a superslick floss. The product, called Glide, doesn't snap, slash gums, or shred between the teeth. Well and good, but how to take on floss giants Johnson & Johnson and Gillette Co.'s Oral-B division? John Spencer, the Gore manager, went for word of mouth in his launch last year. Six months before he hit drugstores, he sent samples to dentists for them to hand out free to patients. "The response was incredible," Spencer says.

Because patients liked the floss, many dentists started buying it. To capture customer names for future product launches, Gore at first sold Glide to the public only through an 800 number. In

Narrowing the Gap

How Big Marketers Can Act as Deftly as Small Companies

Tap the Data Base   Use purchase data to customize incentives and direct-mail based on demographics, location, product preference, and price.

Hire from Smaller Rivals   They excel at "guerrilla marketing"—using local promotions to get close to customers and break through advertising clutter.

Help Your Retailer   Creating store-specific marketing programs—as Dannon does for retailers selling its yogurt—will win retailer loyalty, differentiate your product, and build local sales

...And Small Marketers Can Outwit the Giants

Find the Missed Opportunities   Small marketers can often focus on a relatively neglected product—such as duct tape or dental floss—and take share from a bigger player or increase sales in a tired category.

Apply the Personal Touch   Smaller marketers can get a big payoff when top executives pay personal attention to customers' letters, retailers' queries, and sales staff's suggestions.

Embrace Technology   The cost of data base technology is dropping, making direct-mail marketing a viable tactic for small marketers with tight budgets.

some instances, enthusiasts ordered cases by phone. As a result, Glide had a wide reputation and a core of dedicated users before it hit the stores.

Health Valley Foods, an Irwindale (Calif.) maker of health cereals, soups, and snacks, has been as clever as Gore at out-

flanking big companies by using technology and niche marketing. Started back in 1970, the company at first sold just to
health-food stores. It ignored supermarkets but even so was able
to build an unusually loyal following.

It developed a bond with consumers in several ways: The
founder, George Mateljan, often answered letters of complaint
and inquiry himself, and consumers were able to get friendly
advice on healthy eating by calling an 800 number. The names
all went on a mailing list for special promotions on Health
Valley's growing roster of products. Soon, Health Valley had
enough customer loyalty to move into supermarkets, a remark-
able achievement for an independent operating in a mass-con-
sumption category such as cereal. Since 1989, its sales have doubled, to more than $100 million.

Glide and Health Valley Foods are both rising brands breaking into the crowded marketplace. Dannon, an established
brand, is trying something else. By sharing research with retailers and tailoring marketing to individual chains, it increased
sales 9% through late August, vs. 7% for yogurt overall.

But it's possible, even without deep pockets, to revive a brand
that has lost out. Take Soho Beverages Inc., which Tom Cox, a
former manager at PepsiCo, bought with a partner from liquor
marketer Seagram Co. after Seagram had acquired Soho and
failed to make it thrive. The tiny brand, once a healthy niche
product in New York and a few other places up and down the
East Coast, languished inside Seagram because its sales force
was unused to selling to delis.

By contrast, Cox has managed to boost sales 50%—from a
small base—in the first eight months of 1993. Furthermore, he
has done this on a shoestring budget that doesn't allow for such
strategies as national data-base marketing. "We collect our data
by hand," he says. He hired Korean- and Arabic-speaking college students and had his people walk into practically every
delicatessen in Manhattan in order to reacquaint owners with
the brand, spot consumption trends, and take orders. To create a
new connection with consumers, he sponsored local designated-
driver programs—and offered motorists free Soho Soda in the
bargain. "It's guerrilla marketing," says Cox.

It's also a lesson in not giving up. The U.S. may not be virgin territory for marketers now, as it was back in the days of Clarence Saunders and Michael Cullen. Many consumers, however, still thirst for the new. Even more, they like to feel that they're being listened to. That may be a yearning the shopkeepers of old satisfied best—and one that still holds the secret for marketing success.

By Christopher Power, with Zachary Schiller

6

Finance—
The Floodgates
Inch Open

*Welcome to the new world of small-business
lending. Money is tight—but it can be found.*

Vincent Rua was on the prowl for capital. Over the years, the
president of $15 million Manhattan-based Skyline Windows had
developed good relationships with a number of commercial
banks. But when he went after his 1993 financing, it was an
investment bank that won his business. After reading about
Merrill Lynch Business Financial Services in a newspaper, Rua
called it. "Within 30 days, they had turned around our request
for a $1.25 million line of credit and about $200,000 of capital-
equipment financing," he marvels. "I have dealt with many
banks across the country and in New York, and it's just not
heard of to get a turnaround in 30 days."

Welcome to the changing world of small-business financing.
With President Clinton hailing small business as "the real job-
generating engine of this economy" and many providers of
financial services targeting it as a growth market, there are finally signs of life in the market for small-business lending. Many

banks launching small business-lending initiatives find themselves in competition with other, nontraditional lenders that also
want the business. Last year's record number of venture capital-
backed initial public offerings is drawing more money into venture-capital funds. States are starting programs to encourage
lending. And changes in the taxation of capital gains may spur
more of the wealthy to become "angels"—informal venture capitalists who help many small businesses get their start.

All these new avenues in small-business financing can't come
soon enough for borrowers still feeling the chill of the small-
business credit crunch that began in the mid-1980s. Big losses in
banks' loan portfolios, coupled with tighter regulation, caused
many banks to turn their focus inward, and lending became a
lesser priority. In such a risk-averse environment, only the safest
loans got made. There are still many banks stuck in that mind-
set. "A lot of banks are looking for an airtight deal," says
Kenneth R. Lowe, chief executive officer of $2 million Lowe
Manufacturing Inc., an electronic circuit-board maker based in
Dallas. "Small business is not airtight."

Bankers don't deny that their standards are still tight. More
restrictive policies that lend less against receivables or require
more collateral have drawn complaints that smaller businesses
are paying for others' mistakes. "Banks got so burned by real-
estate deals and bad loans that the companies they've been
doing business with are being punished for the criminals," says
Ted Leonsis, founder of $10.5 million Vero Beach (Fla.)-based
Redgate Communications, which publishes software magazines.

But hope is replacing despair. "There just might be a little cli-
mactic change going on," says Hugh H. Trumbull, president of
$1.4 million Analytical Graphics in Philadelphia. "We have to
earn our spurs every day, but there are signs of good things happening."

One sign that capital is freeing up is the dramatic increase in
loans made through the Small Business Administration. Since
1991, the number of such loans has risen 40%, which produced
$6.4 billion in loans for fiscal 1993. The SBA's up-to-90% guaran-
tee of a loan's value lessens banks' fears about lending to small
companies and opens up the doors to borrowers who don't have
the collateral to get a conventional loan. Even nontraditional

lenders such as American Telephone & Telegraph Co. have begun making SBA-guaranteed loans. AT&T Capital Corp. created the AT&T Small Business Lending Corp. in late 1992 to provide financing to first-time franchisors and other small outfits. "Small businesses are just cropping up everywhere, and for a company to be successful, it certainly can't ignore that marketplace," says Patty Mullane, a spokeswoman for AT&T Capital Corp.

Lenders also open their arms to companies with hard assets, but real-estate loans remain a nightmare. "We're having easier access to borrowing on hard asset-based products than we've ever had," says Walter Riley, president of $35 million Kearny (N.J.)-based Guaranteed Overnight Delivery Inc., a trucking service for oversize packages. Riley is happy with the 5.75% five-year loan he got on $15 million worth of trucks. But don't ask him about his real-estate backed loan. Riley has a balloon payment coming due on an old note, and instead of routinely refinancing it, his New Jersey bank wants to do an appraisal and, suspecting a changed loan-to-value ratio, wants more cash.

Some of the slack in bank lending has been picked up by non-bank lenders. There's Merrill Lynch & Co., which, in a strategic review in 1985, determined that some of its best clients were people who owned their own businesses. After making just $200 in revenues in 1985, its Business Financial Services unit has about $1 billion in revenues today. Its basic product, the Working Capital Management Account, is a combination checking and brokerage account and, for those who qualify, a revolving line of credit. "When you're long on funds, you earn on balances," says Richard A. Hanson, the unit's director. "When you exhaust your funds, you pay us interest." Merrill's accounts hold over $30 billion, mostly for companies that have been in business for at least five years, have $2 million to $25 million in revenues, and have been profitable for the last three years.

Asset-based lenders such as CIT Group Holdings Inc. and Heller Business Credit are also becoming more of a force in the small-business market. Robert D. Keeler found that out when the new management of his bank, which had been acquired, politely told him that it didn't have an appetite for his type of business. So the vice-president of finance for $37 million Cuplex Inc., a Garland (Tex.)-based company in the printed circuit-board business, turned to a trusted adviser at Ernst & Young, who marketed the company to other lenders. Keeler wound up with working capital in excess of what he had with his bank, and says his asset-based lender's formula for lending against inventory and receivables "was less restrictive than the banks and gave us more room for growth."

For startups, though, it never seems to get much easier. "Since 1985, it's been a slippery downward slope, especially for those in early-stage startups," says Jim Fitzsimons, who ran a venture-capital fund for 10 years through Miami's now-defunct Southeast Bank. "Those seeking expansion capital can find it, but the classical entrepreneur today would probably not get funded."

While venture-capital funds are up for the first time since 1987, they favor later-stage investment. Companies under $5 million are finding it very tough, says Michael Puntoriero, partner in Arthur Andersen Enterprise Group's office in Orange County, Calif. Some of his clients go to customers or vendors for financing. But many startups get financed the old-fashioned way, borrowing money from friends and family, mortgaging homes, and drawing on credit cards.

One avenue that may be opening up for early-stage companies is the informal venture-capitalist network. Every year, such self-made "angels" bankroll about 30,000 to 40,000 companies, estimates William E. Wetzel, director of the Center For Venture Research at the University of New Hampshire's Whittemore School of Business & Economics. Wetzel guesses that 250,000 or so angels pump close to $10 billion to $15 billion into early-stage ventures each year.

States are also trying to help small businesses get access to capital. Eager to encourage entrepreneurs with visions of "Silicon-Beach" dancing in their heads, Florida has created Enterprise Florida, billed as a "public-private partnership" with the goal of creating 200,000 jobs by the year 2005. Its first-effort: putting together three $50 million venture-capital fund pools financed by institutions that will cater to TK-stage companies. The state is in the "talking stage" about seed-capital financing, and is looking into creating a "guarantee pool" to enhance fixed-asset financing for growing companies.

Perhaps most cheering are changes in the capital-gains tax. The tax bite is cut by 50% if an individual's investment in a small company is held for five years or longer. "It's Clinton's most promising effort to help the capital market for entrepreneurs," says Wetzel.

There is also action pending on the congressional front. The Small Business Incentive Act of 1993 would make it easier for small businesses to issue securities. The Small Business Capital Enhancement Act calls for the federal and state governments to match funds set aside to cover loan defaults. That could spur banks to lend to less-established or less-creditworthy companies.

Part of the plan on Capitol Hill is to help open the capital markets to small-business loans. That's the motive behind a third act, the Small Business Loan Securitization and Secondary Market Enhancement Act. The act would make it easier for banks to package together small-business loans and treat them much the same as mortgage-backed securities, which have a huge secondary market lenders can sell into. That could make lenders far more willing and able to serve smaller businesses.

With a number of avenues opening up, the odds of getting financing are turning in the entrepreneur's favor. Granted, it may never be easy to get the money to start a small business. But a determined and resourceful entrepreneur can turn to more sources of funding than ever before. And one of them just might be convinced that the smartest investment is in that person's idea.

By Suzanne Woolley, with Janet Lee, Gail DeGeorge,
Stephanie Anderson Forest, and Joy Hainline

7

Finance— Lenders to the Small Fry

They're called microlenders, and they help companies that "probably wouldn't get the time of day in a bank."

Gail Miller, a Dumas (Ark.) potter, had exhausted the bank credit on her six-year-old business. She lost a key employee, ran into an intractable glaze problem, and just couldn't throw enough pots to meet demand for her midpriced dinnerware. Desperate, she turned to Arkansas Enterprise Group (AEG), a nonprofit affiliate of the local Elk Horn Bank & Trust Co. It gave her a $25,000 Small Business Administration loan—and a lot more.

AEG sent a business-service administrator who "came here and sat with me in the mud and got me started with a systematic record," says Miller. AEG sorted out her paperwork and advised her to buy a $19,000 machine that would copy her work exactly. Not a bad idea, considering Miller lost $90,000 last year in unfilled orders. "I can hand-throw 500 pieces a week," Miller says. "This machine can produce 1,500 to 2,000 pieces a week." Now, she looks forward to a time when "it will make me so profitable, I won't know how to act."

Miller joins the growing ranks of the smallest businesses that are surviving, and even thriving, thanks to a nationwide system of grass-roots nonprofit microlenders. Amounting to only a handful five years ago, microlenders now number more than 200. Backed by foundations, governments, banks, and investors, they are meeting a strong demand for loans of less than $25,000—a niche too small for most banks. Moreover, microlenders are trying to bring a more comprehensive approach to helping the poor become self-sufficient.

Most microlenders are three to five years old and have previous lending and business experience. Many target women and minorities. Accion, a Latin American microloan program, serves mainly Hispanics. The Corporation for Enterprise Development (CED) in Washington operates a five-state program in self-employment for welfare recipients.

Borrowers are mostly home-based sole proprietors in retail and service jobs as varied as operating a diaper service or trimming cow hooves. They borrow as little as $50 at rates of 8% to 16%. "Based on their job, credit history, and how little money they want," says SBA spokesman Mike Stamler, "they probably wouldn't get the time of day in a bank." The Small Business Administration gave microlending a boost last year, with a five-year project to lend $75 million to micro centers.

Key to the microloan effort is providing business training. "Technical assistance is as important to most programs as money," says Joyce Klein, a CED program director. Help can mean writing a business plan, computerizing the books, or finding a finer grade of clay. Many centers also have incubators—low-rent office space with access to copiers, supplies, and a receptionist.

Some microfunds use a practice started in India called peer-group lending. Working Capital, in Cambridge, Mass., involves 500 New England concerns in small groups to design and approve each other's loan requests. Repayment is crucial. "If anyone falls behind," says its director, Jeffrey Ashe, "credit for everyone is frozen until the group solves the problem." It's effective: Working Capital has a 98% repayment rate. Peer groups also offer support, advice, and contacts. "It has been excellent," says Nelson Abreu, a Senegalese who lives in North

Bedford, Mass. "We all share each other's experience and the networking has helped." Abreu got $500 to print brochures for his temp-service startup.

Microfunds are having mixed success. Almost none is self-sustaining, mainly because technical assistance is expensive. A study done for the Charles Stewart Mott Foundation of 28 microfunds it backs reveals that 15% to 20% of the outstanding dollar amount was late, and 7.3% was written off last year. (Commercial banks, by comparison, have a charge-off rate of 1% to 2%.) Meanwhile, the $8,134,802 that was lent out financed 2,143 businesses and created 1,733 new nonowner jobs.

Microfunds face many challenges ahead. One is fighting income limits for those on welfare and employment, so they don't lose benefits before they can support themselves off their businesses. Also, efforts to involve banks have gained little ground, with notable exceptions such as Chicago's Shorebank Corp., which has pioneered community development efforts in Chicago's South Side and in Arkansas.

Slumping big-loan business led New England banks into micros. And others in California have made micros pay by streamlining the loan application process and by offering ancillary services. "Entrepreneurs have other banking needs that we're hopefully taking care of as well," says Mike Mantel, president of Bank of America Community Development Bank. "Small businesses," he adds, "become big businesses."

No one knows this better than small community banks, such as BancOne in Columbus, Ohio, where microloans are a mainstay. "We'll work hard to make a $25,000 loan," says spokesperson John Russell. After all, he says, BancOne lent Leslie H. Wexner $10,000 to start The Limited Inc.

By Pam Black

PART 3
Techniques and Trends

8
Letting Go
Is Hard to Do

You're used to giving orders? Well,
empowerment has its rewards, too.

No-nonsense, decisive—even intimidating. That's the way colleagues used to describe Sharon Jacobs, a 39-year-old middle manager at Hewlett-Packard Co. in Santa Clara, Calif. It was by getting results from her people, after all, that she rose to the top of the company's 260-person direct-marketing organization two years ago. No warm and fuzzy mother hen, even Jacobs termed her own style "very authoritarian."

But spurred by pleas from new staffers, Jacobs has undergone a dramatic change in the past two years. After a slow start, she now regards herself as a "sponsor." She asks her telemarketers to suggest solutions when problems arise. And she listens when even lower-level staffers offer ideas. The payoff? Productivity for the unit's key computer-products group is up 40% this year, employee morale has risen sharply enough to draw a note from HP's president, and the unit's annual attrition rate has plunged 44%.

"I set people a much broader charter, and then I say explicitly: 'I trust you,'" explains Jacobs. "It really requires a lot of letting go. [But] they end up delivering far more than the most aggressive goal I ever would have set for them."

All across Corporate America, managers like Jacobs are being forced to let go. Downsizings have gutted corporate ranks, boosting the work load sharply for survivors—particularly middle managers. They're overseeing larger staffs, dealing with far more people who report directly to them, or being forced to delegate to teams of subordinates and colleagues. There's simply too little time to manage in the old tight-fisted way.

But the change doesn't come easily to managers who've climbed the corporate ladder through sheer personal drive and a hands-on style that borders on benevolent despotism. At first, some cling to old ways, working 60-hour weeks to supervise, say, a dozen people who report directly to them instead of the former seven. They rile subordinates—who themselves don't have enough time to baby-sit the boss—and wind up slowing down work. "It is difficult psychologically and philosophically for people to recognize that their role has shifted from being a director and order-giver to becoming more of an educator and motivator," says Ross A. Webber, chairman of the management department at the University of Pennsylvania's Wharton School.

An example from the boss can help. At USF&G Corp., a Baltimore insurer in the midst of a turnaround, CEO Norman P. Blake Jr. makes a point of seeing once a week the dozen people who report to him—at an informal Monday-night dinner. Otherwise, he sees them for a monthly staff meeting and during the week only as needed. His rationale: Let people run their own operations and they'll outperform expectations. "They're not working for somebody as much as running their own businesses," says Blake. But he admits it took six years of seeing consensus-style management work at Japanese-owned Heller International Inc., which he ran in the 1980s, to convince him of the value of teamwork and autonomy.

Experts say the toughest thing for old-style managers to learn is that empowerment doesn't mean abdication. In fact, managers usually take on more responsibility in a team system or a downsized company. It's just the execution that's different, with communication and consensus-building becoming paramount. Noel M. Tichy, a management professor at the University of Michigan, likens the old way to football, a sport where a coach on the sidelines sends in plays and everyone's role is tightly

---

Transformation of the Power Addict

Empowering workers improves corporate performance. But managers accustomed to close oversight often must go through withdrawal. Here's how:

1. **FEAR AND RESISTANCE** At first, managers fear losing control as the number of people reporting to them expands and they lose insulating layers of managers below. So managers stay with what's familiar. Some may feel profound loss.

2. **TENTATIVE ACCEPTANCE** Managers start yielding authority haltingly, clinging to old habits: many meetings, memos, and close policing of subordinates. Result: overwork, buildup of stress, inefficiency. Training programs can drive home the need to accept new ways and build teamwork.

3. **SURRENDER** When they at last see how efficient it is to trust staffers, managers acquiesce. Managers start acting more like coaches than overseers. By letting colleagues help shape policies, managers find people have a stake in their success.

4. **ADVOCACY** As they see colleagues enhance the unit's performance, managers encourage subordinates to share authority even further down the line. Now the subordinates face their own cycle of letting go.

DATA: UNIVERSITY OF MICHIGAN, VANDERBILT UNIVERSITY, BW

---

defined. By contrast, empowered companies operate more like basketball, where, Tichy says, "you have to rely a lot more on real-time improvisation."

Often it takes a crisis to make managers realize that it's time to improvise. Reorganizations that bolster the bottom line typically drive out the managers who can't adapt, and those who are left have no choice but to change. For instance, when J. Michael Bowman joined DuPont Co.'s fibers unit in the mid-

1980s, it was a bloated underperformer. Since then, downsizings have trimmed several thousand jobs, and the unit has been restructured into a $6 billion-a-year group of free-standing businesses that have empowered their workers. Today they contribute more than a quarter of DuPont's earnings, even though many of their markets are mired in slow growth.

Surprisingly, Bowman had no problem shedding the "command-and-control" style that marked 20 of his 28 years at DuPont. "People have more freedom, but they have more responsibility," he says. So, he's pushing autonomy more than ever at the advanced-materials business he now runs for the company. "Some people love that," he says, "and to some it's a shock."

Training programs can minimize that shock. Consultants like Tichy take managers off on rope-climbing or mountain-scaling expeditions, where the real purpose is to build trust among team members. Other companies such as CSX Corp. push subordinates to develop after-hours camaraderie. "You really have to feel comfortable with the individual you are giving responsibility to," explains M. McNeil Porter, CEO of the $825 million-a-year CSX Intermodal unit.

Managers also have to realize that once empowerment takes hold, it's not easily cast aside. At Boeing Co., supervisor Mike Ralston once asked a group of workers in a parts-storage area to plan a move to a new building. When moving day came, Ralston promptly told the workers what to haul over first. "They came unglued," he recalls. "They asked me: 'Why are you making a decision? We've worked on this for six months.' I was shocked." It turned out that Ralston had learned that certain critical parts had to be in place early. Belatedly, he explained why in a 45-minute chat, and they came around. But he recalls: "I owed it to them to share with them what I knew."

Managers who yield control to empowered staffers usually became the strongest advocates of the approach. At Bell Atlantic Corp., Assistant Vice-President Thomas M. Podesta oversees about 1,400 people in bill processing and payroll. Once, his job was done by six people in three operating companies. Now he does it alone, and most of his subordinates police their own work.

Managers who share power have to learn another tough lesson: developing a tolerance for mistakes. Staffers sometimes have to see a project go awry to prevent similar foul-ups in the future. That's often difficult. Admits Boeing's Ralston: "There were times when I had to walk around the building rather than intervene."

So empowerment doesn't mean the end of supervision. Instead, it requires managers to take less pride in their own accomplishments and more in those of the staff they oversee. That kind of new attitude shift can't be forced on managers. But even a recalcitrant boss can learn to let go when he or she sees results.

By Joseph Weber, with Dori Jones Yang

9

Turning Rivals into Teammates

Little outfits have the fresh ideas. Big companies have the bucks. So why not join forces?

By 1990, it was crunch time for Ford Motor Co. The nation's second-largest carmaker could no longer sidestep investing more than $200 million to create a new diesel engine for its midsize trucks. After all, tough 1994 U.S. emission standards loomed, and the technology needed would require a big research effort. But Ford, pouring cash into its ailing auto business, didn't want to throw money at another problem.

So Ford hit on a novel approach. It plunked down $100 million for a 10% stake in Cummins Engine Co., which had developed a clean-burning diesel. The move handed Cummins both a long-term customer and more cash to continue its expensive research into next-generation technologies. Today, Ford is buying from Cummins more than 30,000 midrange engines, which helped the once-ailing engine maker post earnings of $89.3 million, on sales of $2.1 billion during the first half of 1993.

Ford isn't alone. Across Corporate America, partnerships between giants such as Ford and smaller companies like Cummins are spreading like a prairie fire. This summer, American

Airlines Inc. turned the unprofitable short-haul operations at its
San Jose (Calif.) hub over to low-cost Reno Air Inc., which will
feed traffic to the larger carrier. Drug companies such as Eli
Lilly, Merck, and SmithKline are forging bonds with pharmaceutical startups to gain access to their path-breaking technologies. Manufacturers Motorola, DuPont, and Caterpillar are cozy-
ing up to suppliers, looking to cut costs by tapping their
product design and manufacturing expertise. Says Deborah
Wince-Smith, a senior fellow at the Council on Competitiveness:
"Big companies have realized it isn't smart to go it alone in a
global market."

Indeed, the impetus to partnership can be summed up in one
word: competitiveness. Global competition, coupled with the
supersonic pace of innovation, has compelled large companies to
play every angle to survive. IBM, Ford, and General Motors have
found that to cut costs or keep up with technological shifts they
need the help of little guys. Small dynamos, free of the bureaucracy that hampers many big companies, often hit on new products, markets, or designs first. "Big companies don't do this to
think small," notes consultant Jordan Lewis, who helps companies forge partnerships. "Large companies partner with small
ones because the small company has something they want."

Still, the best large companies approach partnerships with a
much broader agenda. Some want help cutting costs. Others
want a jump-start developing new technologies. Still others
want a window onto niche markets that they normally would
overlook.

Manpower International, the $3.2 billion temporary-employ-
ment-services company, for instance, established in 1993 a
national partnership with a $50 million black-owned company
to allow Manpower to tap the U.S. minority labor pool better.
Many Manpower customers want to diversify their work forces,
including staffers hired through Manpower. "The alternative
would have been to look around in each market for minority
vendors, which would have been inefficient and couldn't guarantee us quality nationwide," explains CEO Mitchell S.
Fromstein.

But while many big service companies are just now recogniz-
ing the benefits of partnership, manufacturers have been converts for years. In the late 1970s, big companies saddled with

high-priced union contracts, such as Ford, Deere, and Caterpillar, started diverting more work to suppliers to cut labor costs. Later, as suppliers provided more and more of the value of a product—up to 50% in autos—industrial giants had to build tighter links to their suppliers to boost quality and lower costs further.

They weren't alone. To boost their own growth rates, large pharmaceutical companies over the past 20 years have dramatically increased their licensing partnerships with small startups that have developed promising drugs.

It's not just the big boys that benefit in these couplings. Partnering with a behemoth such as DuPont, IBM, or Caterpillar also has advantages for those small or lucky enough to get tapped. Take Morton Metalcraft Co., a Morton (Ill.) sheet-metal fabricator with $30 million in sales. Three years ago, the company began cozying up to construction-equipment giant Caterpillar, Inc., which initially farmed out some metal bending work to Morton in a bid to cut costs.

Gradually, Caterpillar entrusted more responsibility for product design to Morton, which could do the job better and cheaper, says CEO William Morton. As a result, Morton's sales to Caterpillar are growing more than 10% annually, says Morton. Caterpillar hasn't done shabbily either. When the partners teamed up to tackle cost problems, improvements in excess of 10% have been common.

But partnering isn't easy. A not-invented-here mentality still dominates most corporate giants. And even well-conceived partnerships are fraught with opportunities for failure. Why? Despite the successes trumpeted by the likes of Xerox, Corning, and DuPont, big company research and engineering departments greet warily most innovations generated by suppliers and small-company partners. Moreover, what many corporations call partnering remains simply an old-fashioned effort to extract price concessions from suppliers. Says Kenneth Stork, former Motorola Inc. purchasing chief: "When someone suggests a partnership to me, my hand still automatically moves to protect my wallet."

The high-profile efforts by GM and General Electric Co. to cut costs by demanding price reductions from suppliers certainly reinforced this view. Suppliers to GE's appliance division were invited to partner with the unit in exchange for 10% annual price reductions. "They didn't care how much cost you had already taken out," grouses one GE supplier. "It was patently unfair." Similarly, GM's former purchasing guru, José Ignacio López de Arriortua, tore up long-term contracts and demanded price reductions from suppliers. The controversial effort, says GM, saved the company $4 billion on parts.

But overemphasis on cutting component prices is a rationale many U.S. companies are trying to leave behind. "Corporations are finding there's only just so much blood you can squeeze," says James P. Kuhn, a vice-president at consultants A. T. Kearney Inc. Instead, manufacturers are increasingly forging long-term relationships with suppliers to work together as a team to hack away at costs, often sharing the savings.

Take Chrysler Corp. When it started designing its Neon sub-compact in 1990, it involved 25 key suppliers. They helped engineer the car and negotiated target prices for parts up-front, allowing them to design for cost containment. The result: Development took three years, compared with an industry average of five, and cost just $1.3 billion. By contrast, GM's Saturn cost $5 billion.

One hotbed for partnering has been the drug industry, where established manufacturers such as Merck & Co. increasingly rely on small companies for new-product ideas to augment their own research efforts. Frank Baldino, president of Cephalon Inc., a West Chester (Pa.) startup that spends most of its funds on research, says: "Why not hook up with us, and do it for 10% of the cost?"

That's happening more and more. For example, two years ago Eli Lilly & Co. needed a way to deliver drugs to prevent heart blockage from recurring after an angioplasty, a procedure used to open blocked arteries, which has become a booming business for Lilly's medical-device division. Meanwhile, Zynaxis Inc., a Malvern (Pa.) startup, had a drug-delivery system but needed a deep-pocketed partner to help with the clinical trials, which can cost up to $200 million.

So a partnership was struck. For a $3 million investment in Zynaxis and a further $1.26 million a year to speed research, Lilly secured the technology. Although a product is still a few years off, says Lilly director of drug-delivery devices Robert W. Scott, early signs are promising.

Even with all the success stories, partnering remains a stretch for many corporations. The need to build mutual trust often conflicts with their standard operating procedures. It's essential, therefore, says former Motorola purchasing chief Stork, to build a corporate culture that values cooperation and to communicate constantly.

At Motorola, for instance, former Chief Executive Robert W. Galvin used to make presentations about the importance of close relations with suppliers. And executives at DuPont Co. meet quarterly with managers at Milwaukee-based W. H. Brady Co. to set goals for their partnership, which sells a jointly developed product used to post ads on the sides of trucks. Project teams of lower-level workers meet even more often, says William Hayes, Brady's general manager.

Obviously, building partnerships takes time. But where corporations such as Ford and Caterpillar have made the effort to find capable teammates, the gains have been unmistakable. Indeed, while thinking small may be the order of the day in America's big companies, sometimes it's enough to just find a partner—albeit a smaller one.

By Kevin Kelly, with Wendy Zellner, Eric Schine, and James E. Ellis

10

How Goliaths Can Act like Davids

More giants are working to combine the clout of bigness with the human scale and sharp focus of smallness.

Donald G. Berger speaks with the exhaustion and excitement of an entrepreneur who has labored for years over a potentially world-beating product. The prelaunch series of 20-hour days, the roller coaster of emotions, the anxiety about whether sophisticated systems would whir, and finally, the champagne-toasts—he has been through it all. "This is a once-in-a-lifetime opportunity," gushes Berger, the new chief executive officer of Roadway Global Air Inc. in Indianapolis. "We've brought a new company to market, not just in the U.S. but globally."

Yet the mid-September, 1993, takeoff of Global Air, which aimed to bring new standards of high-tech service to the international package-delivery business, is no ordinary venture deal. Instead, it's the latest and boldest startup spawned by Global Air's 63-year-old parent, $3.7 billion transportation giant Roadway Services Inc. As was the case with Roadway's earlier moves beyond old-line, long-distance trucking into such fields as small-package delivery, Roadway is flying into a low-margin business that has well-entrenched competitors, including Burlington Air Express, Emery Worldwide, and DHL. And it figures to spend at least $100 million before Global Air sees any black ink.

No matter. Extensive research points to unsatisfied customers. So now, Roadway is betting that its new company-within-a-company, staffed by inspired employees, can fulfill the lofty dreams of any startup. "We may be in the overnight business, but we aren't going to build a global power overnight," notes Berger, who was lured from a 22-year career at Consolidated Freightways by the prospect of building his own company. "But Roadway is willing to stick with this."

Patient, nimble, and innovative. Not exactly characteristics usually associated with the trucking industry—or many big companies, for that matter. Rather, it's the sickly hulks of IBM, General Motors, and Westinghouse that have led employees, customers, capital markets, and the media to demonize much of Big Industry while reserving a special place in their hearts for blossoming small companies.

Well, look again. There are scores of Roadways stirring around the globe. They are quietly embarking on a bold adventure to combine the advantages of bigness—access to capital, formidable research capabilities, and global-marketing and distribution reach—with the human scale, sharp focus, and fervent entrepreneurship of smallness.

In industries as diverse as measuring instruments and hotels, pharmaceuticals and retailing, companies are slicing themselves into more manageable pieces, farming out all but essential functions, sharing risks with new partners, and once again listening to their customers. They also are employing technology to act quickly and strike a competitive advantage, whether it's retailing giant May Department Stores Co.'s mastery of computers to monitor inventories or Roadway's promise of real-time tracking of myriad packages.

Above all, the best of the big are seeking something quite basic: to make their companies attractive places to work. Through stock options, customer-satisfaction bonuses, or opportunities to create businesses, big enterprises are trying to bind their interests more intimately with those of their workers.

Herbert D. Kelleher, co-founder and cheerleading CEO of Southwest Airlines Inc., can credit much of the carrier's astonishing success to never having strayed far from the feel of a mom-and-pop outfit—even as $1.7 billion Southwest has grown into the nation's eighth largest airline.

To maintain the buzz, the iconoclastic Kelleher—who has dressed as Elvis and the Easter bunny on flights—has deployed everything from traditional profit-sharing schemes to a buddy system linking old and new employees. As a result, Southwest is not only the U.S. airline industry's most consistent profit-spinner but also a company that will attract 100 applications for each vacancy this year. Credit, in part, Kelleher's strikingly simple mantra: "Think and act small, and we'll be bigger. Think and act big, and we'll get smaller."

Such plain-spoken advice was widely ignored in much of Corporate America, as well as Europe and Asia, over the past decade in a mad dash for size. No longer. Beginning in Britain and now spreading across much of Europe, recession-wracked companies are rewriting social contracts that guaranteed generous employee benefits, shifting jobs to low-wage countries, and, sometimes, even shuttering businesses.

This summer, Britain's largest manufacturer, Imperial Chemical Industries PLC, spun off its highly profitable drug unit, Zeneca PLC, from its basic chemical interests into a separate company with its own stock. German stalwarts Daimler Benz, Siemens, and Volkswagen are laying off tens of thousands of workers in a furious, if risky, attempt to remake a culture that has changed little since the early postwar era.

Half a world away, large Japanese companies such as Ricoh, Mitsubishi Electric, and Nippon Telephone & Telegraph are equally intent on trimming their bloated organizations. Because of cultural differences, the methods used are often more subtle. Toyota Motor Corp. will hire only half the workers originally planned, while Digital Equipment Corp. in Japan is requesting that 200 employees seek voluntary early retirement. But the results will be the same: trimmer Japanese giants that can better compete with companies that don't carry so much bureaucratic baggage.

There's danger in simply chopping heads without having a

broader plan to change the way the remaining organization operates. Just look at IBM, Eastman Kodak, or General Motors, all groping giants that discovered to their chagrin that mass firings can merely erode morale, leaving the skinnier company no more coherent than before. "The advantages to head-count cuts is that they happen fast, and the markets tend to react favorably," notes Kim S. Cameron, a professor at the University of Michigan business school. "The disadvantage is that it's like throwing a grenade into a crowded room." And Cameron has seen the fallout: Of the 150 restructuring companies he has studied, three-quarters end up worse off after their downsizing.

Of course, many smaller companies have gone astray, just like big ones. And often it's for the same reasons: They build in too much bureaucracy as they get larger, and lose touch with their employees and principal markets.

Yet the job-creating power and financial returns of the healthiest small companies highlight a big gap between them and their larger counterparts. It also comes down to the bottom line: In terms of operating income per employee before depreciation, America's top-performing small public companies outperform the corporate giants in scores of industries, at rates ranging from 1.4 times better in general manufacturing to a staggering 5.1 times in computer software and services, according to Standard & Poor's Compustat Services Inc.

The best of the big—companies such as General Electric, Emerson Electric, and Johnson & Johnson, with their heavy emphasis on small management teams running highly decentralized units—have rarely lost sight of the virtues of smallness. Others, including communication giants American Telephone & Telegraph Co. and Motorola Inc., have been traumatized into remaking themselves by deregulation, heavy international competition, or both. Still others, such as $2 billion luxury hotelier Hyatt Hotels Corp., have only recently accepted the need to overhaul themselves to deal with the slowed growth and tight-fisted customers of the 1990s.

Whatever the reason for their conversion, big companies that think small share a realization that maintaining the flexibility of a small enterprise—not sheer size—will be the real measure of their long-term success. "Boards and managements that have been focused so heavily on short-term financial results are now attacking what makes their companies great for the long term," says Cyrus F. Freidheim Jr., vice-chairman of consultant Booz, Allen & Hamilton Inc.

One place to start is to break the behemoth into far more manageable units, structured around product lines or discrete businesses. Such moves can unleash a tidal wave of payoffs as companies accelerate the development of products and unleash the pent-up creativity of their employees.

Just ask Emerson Chief Executive Officer Charles F. Knight, whose $8.2 billion precision instrument manufacturer has logged a stunning 36 consecutive years of record earnings from his 40 highly autonomous—but highly accountable—divisions.

Knight uses three quick measures to determine whether big companies have become lumbering and bureaucratic. He argues that the best companies will push the planning and control of profits down to product lines. They will ruthlessly avoid building up headquarters staff, which at Emerson is at the same level as 10 years ago, despite a doubling of sales. And they will open communication channels so that crucial competitive and financial information flows down to the shop floor and suggestions flow up from there to the chairman. Knight, for instance, says he personally reviews every opinion survey from Emerson's 233 plants.

Knight is about to get a chance to apply those tests at America's most troubled big company, IBM, where he has recently become a board member. He's no Pollyanna when it comes to what's necessary to make Big Blue or any other big company more flexible. "It sounds easy, but it requires a complete change in how people act and think to move away from a large centralized organization," he explains.

That's why the best of the big companies frequently resemble nothing so much as a collection of small ones. By stripping out—or refusing to add—layers of management, they sidestep what Dartmouth College business professor James Brian Quinn calls "excessive rationalism"—a common pitfall that leads big companies to build in so much analysis and planning that they simply avoid taking risks.

For a primer on how to do it right, look at Johnson & Johnson. This $14 billion health-care giant, a perennial industry leader in profits and innovation, is really a group of 168 companies selling everything from Band-Aids and birth-control pills to baby powder and Tylenol. If one of its dozens of labs develops a hot product, a new company is created to peddle it.

American auto-parts maker Dana Corp., a big supplier to big U.S., European, and Japanese carmakers, has applied this small-is-beautiful approach to its far-more prosaic business. Only a handful of Dana's 120 plants employ more than 200 people, and when a division of the $5 billion company gets too big, it simply gets split in half. "Plant managers should know the name and personal circumstances of everyone," insists Dana Chairman Southwood J. Morcott.

Many conglomerates, of course, are being driven by competitors and capital markets to even more extreme solutions. Now that managers extol the virtues of focus instead of the safety of a diversified business portfolio, they are lopping off big limbs. For companies as diverse as American Express, Textron, and Sears Roebuck, it's back to basics—which almost always means a concentration on a smaller, more manageable group of businesses.

Often, the result is far better performance, both at the spin-offs and the parent companies. Investment bankers Mitchell & Co. looked at 10 representative conglomerates that spun off units in recent years, and discovered their share prices after five years were 39% higher than the Standard & Poor's 500-stock index.

In fact, most big companies have discovered something small companies knew all along: They can't do it all. More and more activities that have no payoff are being off-loaded.

As part of its reconstructive surgery from disabling loan losses, Continental Bank Corp. pushed almost everything not tied to lending and trading money—food and legal services, building maintenance, even its information systems management—to outside suppliers. And Sun Microsystems, a $4.3 billion maker of computer workstations, recently closed its distribution warehouses and turned worldwide shipping over to such companies as Federal Express and Nippon Express.

"Given today's margins in the computer business, we need to take our scarce resources and apply them to areas that will get us faster to market and get us the technologies we need," says Sun Microsystems Vice-President Robert Graham.

For Sun Microsystems and scores of other companies, the not-invented-here syndrome, which has slowed so many large companies' response time, may be a thing of the past. Today, big companies such as Hewlett-Packard and Sweden's L. M. Ericsson are teaming up with their smaller brethren in a rush to spread risks, enter new markets quickly, and relearn entrepreneurial tricks.

Even mammoth AT&T, which recently showed its prodigious financial muscle by plunking down $12.6 billion to buy cellular kingpin McCaw Cellular Communications Inc., sees its limits. That's one reason it's joining Apple, Sony, Philips, Matsushita, and Motorola in backing tiny startup General Magic's quest to develop wireless communications software.

But the answer isn't always outside. Companies such as 3M, AT&T, and Texas Instruments are now serving as beacons for others seeking to unleash entrepreneurs and new ventures within multibillion-dollar enterprises.

One way is to encourage research and development labs or planning staffs to incubate projects that can be run almost as experiments outside more mature units—and to single them out for special notice. 3M, for example, allows employees to set aside 15% of their work week for new-project ideas. The most promising notions can evolve into work teams and new divisions. And the idea generators can reap handsome rewards, from $50,000 "genius grants" to merit raises and profit-sharing.

For all of the big-company rethinking under way, however, the critical issue is how to recapture the type of allegiance and commitment that have long been hallmarks of the best small outfits. Big-company managers increasingly recognize the symbiotic relationship between inspired employees and the bottom line. And a surprisingly simple way for companies to inspire workers is often just to listen to them. That's tough for many managers, simply because they might not like what they hear.

Employees at Hyatt Hotels, for example, are actively encouraged to question orders that come down from the hotelier's Chicago headquarters—and they regularly redraft roughly 70% of the edicts, notes President Darryl Hartley-Leonard. "We refer to the field [employees] as the loyal opposition," jokes the hotelier.

But there are plenty of benefits from an open dialogue with workers to salve management's bruised egos. Hyatt's successful new "Camp Hyatt" and "Rock Hyatt" programs, for children and teens at its resorts, were spawned by an employee suggestion. And Hyatt has helped finance employee startups in such areas as restaurant management and event planning, occasionally subcontracting work back to them.

Once senior managers begin to listen to their work force, rather than simply talking down, it's not long before many consider changes in another area that can make employees true partners: compensation. Schemes such as stock options, quality bonuses, and raises pegged to customer satisfaction are proliferating at big companies. A recent study of 2,000 companies by consultants Hewitt Associates reveals that 68% of them have incentive programs that extend throughout the business, up from 44% five years ago. By the year 2000, predicts Hewitt Director Ed Guberman, virtually all companies will have such plans.

And there's growing evidence of quick payback. An American Compensation Assn. study found that companies are earning back twice what they are paying out in employee incentives, thanks to increased productivity and sales.

At heavy manufacturer Harnischfeger Corp. in Milwaukee, for example, CEO Jeffrey T. Grade deploys five incentive plans for different employee levels. The most novel links the salaries of 500 managers to the return on assets they manage. "It makes these people feel like small store owners," says Grade.

Longer term, big companies must practice a delicate balancing act that allows autonomy at the lowest levels possible while maintaining the advantages that size can bestow. Emerson Electric, for example, recently discovered it had 15 die-casting operations scattered among its autonomous divisions, a needless duplication. So the company plans to turn over all of those operations to an outside supplier in which Emerson will take a stake.

However, having to fix such unexpected inefficiencies later is a small price to pay for the gains that corporate giants generate by empowering both managers and workers. After all, as General Electric Co. Chairman John F. Welch Jr. notes, no company starts out intending to stay small forever. The trick is continuing to think small as you grow.

By Richard A. Melcher, with Wendy Zellner, and Robert D. Hof

11

Entrepreneurship around the World

Russia: Hurdles include public disdain, red tape, hit men.

Deep in a forest outside Moscow, a sprawling pink mansion is in the midst of renovation. Workers are refurbishing all the rooms, including putting Italian marble on the bathroom walls. The dacha was once the weekend hideaway of such Communist leaders as Leonid Brezhnev and Andrei Gromyko. It will soon become the headquarters of Arter Group, a company with 2,000 employees and interests ranging from mining and energy to banking and real estate. The owner of the company and the house is one Andrey Chuguyevsky, a skinny, 35-year-old former history teacher who is today one of Russia's most successful entrepreneurs.

In the chaos following the collapse of the Soviet empire, "biznezmen" such as Chuguyevsky are spawning hundreds of companies, a commercial banking system, and thousands of retail stores that provide decent goods to long-starved consumers. Just a few years ago, such activity was illegal. Some, including Chuguyevsky, got prison sentences.

Not that it's any picnic today. Entrepreneurs face huge taxes, shakedowns from government regulators, and—occasionally—murder from hit men hired by competitors. Instead of being admired as bold Horatio Algers, they are generally reviled by a public struggling along on low, fixed salaries while inflation rages at 30% a month.

Yet many of Russia's young nouveaux riches are not entrepreneurs at all. They are merely traders scarfing up oil and metals and peddling them overseas for a quick buck. They have already provoked crackdowns by the Russian government and by the European Community, which has ordered sanctions against Russia for aluminum dumping. "What's important is that the entrepreneur actually produces something," says Sergei Olevsky, a Moscow scientist-turned-entrepreneur.

He and Chuguyevsky got their big breaks in the late 1980s, when Mikhail Gorbachev revived cooperatives, or small private businesses. A former microelectronics researcher, Olevsky started a cooperative in 1988 that made computer controls. Now, his empire includes three banks, a tourism company, 12 clothing factories, and Tiana, a company that makes shampoo and cosmetics from natural ingredients. Today, Olevsky can easily afford tuition at the University of Pittsburgh for his son, who plans to major in economics. For entrepreneurs, education is critical, Olevsky believes: "We have fine mathematicians and physicists. But we need people who can understand business and economics."

There's plenty of irony, too, in Chuguyevsky's career path. Just 10 years ago, he was a history teacher in Chita, a region on the Chinese border. Future prospects seemed dim, so he and a partner looked elsewhere. When factory managers moaned about their primitive telephone systems, the men put together a team of moonlighting engineers to produce homemade switching systems. The switches sold like hotcakes. But they also attracted the attention of the police. "I asked the woman who arrested us what we were guilty of. She answered: 'The criminal code is big. We'll find something,'" says Chuguyevsky. He got a two-year sentence. His partner got five years.

When Chuguyevsky got out of jail, Gorbachev was just about to permit cooperatives. Chuguyevsky moved to Moscow and started selling personal computers made in Taiwan and

Singapore. He dabbled for a whole in trying to locate and market Russian technologies. Aside from some pollution-control devices his engineers developed for a Ukrainian oil refinery, the results were not promising. "I learned that we are one generation behind on applied research," says Chuguyevsky.

Today, Arter Group has holdings in banking and real estate—and plans projects in gold, coal, and timber. Perhaps, as in earlier capitalist societies, the wealth created through exploitation of natural resources will help spawn the technologically advanced industries the former Soviet Union needs to compete on a global scale. When—or if—that happens, it is likely to be entrepreneurs such as Chuguyevsky who lead the way.

By Peter Galuszka

Chile: Entrepreneurs are one key to Chile's impressive growth.

The world's only scented children's footwear, Manuel Mrquez believes, is turned out by his Calzados Dolphitos plant in Santiago. Brisk demand from kids and parents for the brightly colored shoes and sneakers, exuding such odors as strawberry, watermelon, and chocolate, pushed the 10-year-old company's sales to $14 million last year, up from $6 million in 1986 when Mrquez launched his fragrant product line.

With a home market of only 14 million people, Mrquez until recently got nearly half his revenues from exports. This year, handicapped by an overvalued peso, exports will fall to $3 million, down from $6.3 million in 1992. But Mrquez, who started working in a shoe factory at age 16, has combined imaginative footwear with fast business footwork. Next month, a joint venture with Zaria, a privatized Russian shoemaker, will start producing his footwear in Moscow. "From there, we can break into the European market more easily, with cheaper freight and labor costs," Mrquez says.

Mrquez is one of thousands of entrepreneurs who are diversifying Chile's economy away from commodities such as copper and wood pulp into value-added products, from furniture to biotechnology. They have helped drive Chile's fast economic growth—an average 7% annual expansion of gross national product over the last five years. This year, Chileans are creating 20,000 companies, says Enrique Romn, head of a government development agency—more than any South American country save Brazil, which is 10 times Chile's size.

Chile's two decades of free-market reforms have unshackled entrepreneurs. Bank credit is plentiful, fed by a high savings rate. And government credits and technical aid to startups will rise to $600 million this year, up from $300 million in 1992. "To sustain 6% growth, you need a steady stream of small and mid-size projects," Romn says.

Startups still face some hurdles, from red tape to the lack of tax breaks for venture capital. But conditions for entrepreneurs were tougher 10 years ago when Mrquez, now 49, decided to make shoes on his own after working for Canada's Bata Industries Ltd. in Chile, Canada, and Mexico. Facing a flood of cheap Asian imports, Mrquez realized he had to make his shoes stand out in the market. Complaints of friends about their kids' smelly shoes led him to add scents.

"There's a lot of people who think big," Mrquez says. "I bring the ideas down to earth." To do so, he plows 5% of sales into research and development. "Other companies are always copying our ideas, so we have to keep innovating," Mrquez says. His newest niche product, to be launched in October, will be shoes with lights that flash at each step.

For quite a few Chilean enterprises, the catalyst has been the nonprofit Chile Foundation (FC), set up in 1976 to help spur new ventures, partly by promoting technology transfers. It is funded equally by ITT Corp. and the government, which paid off ITT's prior claims for expropriated properties on condition that ITT plow the money back into the foundation. A decade ago, FC helped launch two salmon farms using techniques from the U.S. and Scandinavia. This year, dozens of Chilean fish farms will product 65,000 tons of salmon. And the aquaculture boom has spread to other seafoods, from turbot to scallops.

"The foundation accelerated a process that would have taken place anyway," says FC General Director Anthony Wylie. "Now, people are moving in for themselves. And they finally believe that technology in Chile can be profitable." A still-blossoming example is software. This year, small companies will sell $40 million worth of software abroad, up from $1.5 million in 1991.

Small businesses will get a boost from a law to be passed by Chile's Congress in October, allowing big privatized pension funds to invest 10% of their money in venture-capital funds, up from 5% at present. And the government proposes to set up a one-stop agency to speed new ventures through the bureaucratic maze. Such measures should help keep the engine of entrepreneurship driving Chile's rapid growth.

By Alexandra Huneeus

12

Small Business and the Japanese Experience

Corporate socialism gives way to greater individual initiative, fewer automatic promotions, and pink slips.

Hironobu Yagata confronted a frightening reality last June. Audio and video gear built by his division at Sanyo Electric Co. were rapidly losing competitiveness as the yen soared and production costs at home remained intractable. As president of Sanyo's A/V Business Headquarters, Yagata knew the only solution was to shift as much of his manufacturing as possible from Japan to lower-cost countries such as Malaysia and China—and the sooner the better.

Until last year, making such a decision would have required months of consensus-building throughout the company in time-honored Japanese management fashion. Yagata, like most Japanese managers, simply lacked the authority to make quick decisions. So he would need to consult scores of product and strategic planners, people in the trading and sales divisions, overseas production managers, as well as top Sanyo managers before making changes.

No longer. Thanks to a "no excuse" decentralized management structure adopted by Sanyo last year, Yagata quickly consulted with several key executives who would be directly affected by the decision. Then, he drafted the reasons for his plan and its anticipated results and informed all concerned of his decision. He alone assumed responsibility for his decision, ultimately saving Sanyo from costly delays during a time when swift action was critical to the bottom line. By 1996, 70% of the TVs Sanyo sells in Japan will be made abroad, more than double current levels. And 90% of its audio products for the domestic market will come from off-shore, compared with 70% now.

What may sound like routine decision-making in a Western company constitutes no less than a revolution-in-the-making at dozens of top-heavy, over-manned companies that got fat during Japan's rapid-growth "bubble years." Now, mired in recession and faced with heightened competition from such rapidly developing countries as South Korea and Taiwan—and even from resurgent U.S. industry—Japanese companies are bent on slimming down, delayering management, and delegating more responsibility to individual executives. Indeed, a recent survey of 250 big companies by Tokyo's Industrial Labor Research Institute found that 49.6% of them plan to reduce management ranks.

"Japanese companies are now going through the restructuring that U.S. companies have been going through for the past 10 years," says George B. Graen, director of the Center for the Enhancement of International Competitiveness at the University of Cincinnati. "They are starting to wonder if they can continue to afford the cultural costs of their way of doing business."

This tougher line is sending shock waves throughout Japanese society. Such sacred cows as lifetime employment at major companies, automatic promotion, and avoidance of individual responsibility can no longer be taken for granted. It's a trauma difficult for Westerners to understand, thanks to Japan's unique culture and social imperatives.

Unlike Americans, who prize individualism and risk-taking, Japanese are raised to think of themselves first as members of a group. The common interest takes precedence over individual initiative and accomplishment. What's more, most Japanese derive their identity mainly from where they work. And management's priority is to provide secure jobs. If that hurts profits, so be it.

This sclerotic employment policy was essential as labor-starved Japan rebuilt itself after World War II. The policy was perpetuated by Japanese employers who invested unusually large amounts to train workers they didn't want to lose. But as competition mounts, Japan's economy matures, and Japanese companies globalize, such traditions as consensus decision-making and automatic promotions based on age and seniority are becoming luxuries Japan can ill afford.

Focusing on white-collar efficiency is important because, despite rapid growth, overall productivity in Japan still trails America's by about 25%. Most of this lag stems from the inefficient service sector and bloated staffs at manufacturers. Between 1976 and 1990, for example, the cost of sales administration at publicly-traded companies in Japan rose from 12.3% of sales to 16.3%, according to the Japan Productivity Center.

Kuniyoshi Sasaki, director of the center's research institute, blames this on a proliferation of "useless" jobs aimed at accommodating baby boomers gaining seniority. This practice was affordable during the go-go days but has become difficult to stop in lean times, because huge numbers of boomers were hired 25 years ago with the implicit promise of ever-upward promotions. "Jobs here are less clearly defined than elsewhere," Sasaki says. "Companies first hire people and then think about what job they can do. Layers grow, and networks get very complicated."

Such executives as Sanyo Electric President Yasuaki Takano are out to correct this. During the past two years, Takano has slashed the number of headquarters departments to 17 from 36, reducing the staff count to 1,350 from 1,700. By 1995, he plans to trim his payroll through attrition to 27,000 people from the current 30,600. Takano has also restructured the company into eight divisions, each headed by a "president" who is accountable for everything from sales and production to capital investment. "We treat them as separate companies," says Takano. "They each have their own profit-and-loss statement and balance sheet. We'll have to fire those who can't get the job done."

Sanyo is far from alone. Two years ago, faced with its first-ever losses, office equipment maker Ricoh Co. cloistered eight executives in a Tokyo hotel room for three days of meetings to forge a restructuring plan. The result: Ricoh will cut its 14,000 payroll by 28% by 1996, including slashing half its headquarters staff by 1995. It also is assigning 500 white-collar workers at a time to four-month stints on production lines to reduce the need for part-time workers.

Likewise, to minimize costs and make white-collar employees more market-conscious, Matsushita Electric Industrial Co. is about to start assigning 1,000 middle managers and 1,000 new college graduate employees to work in company-affiliated stores. Matsushita continues to pay their salaries. Other companies, such as Asahi Mutual Life Insurance Co., take such stop-gap steps as reducing overtime by turning out the lights at 5 p.m. on designated days and locking the copy machines of sections that exceed their photocopy budgets.

Thus far, no large employer has resorted to mass layoffs or firings. Doing so would shatter the social contract. So corporations that need to shed more workers faster than attrition allows are reassigning managers over a certain age, usually 50, to subsidiaries. That basically shifts the bureaucracy to less visible parts of the economy—but ones that needn't worry as much about international cost competitiveness.

Other employers such as Nippon Telegraph & Telephone Corp. and IBM Japan Ltd. are adopting voluntary early-retirement plans. These aren't as popular as in the U.S., however, because retirees lose the status of their former jobs. Also, the relative lack of venture capital and the lower regard for entrepreneurship in Japan mean that few see early retirement as an opportunity to start their own businesses.

Solving this lack of entrepreneurial instincts will be key to the full success of Japan's corporate restructurings. Indeed, making individual managers more accountable won't achieve much unless they're also made to think more creatively, take initiative, and assume risk.

"Future management has to put more emphasis on individuality to get the kind of innovation that we'll need," says Yoshio Maruta, chairman of Kao Corp., a leading maker of household and personal-care products. That will test some deeply ingrained cultural attitudes. But Japanese can be quick learners and resourceful survival artists. Just ask Hironobu Yagata.

By Robert Neff, with James E. Ellis

13

Percy Barnevik's Global Crusade at ABB

ABB's chief has broken the global giant into 5,000 profit centers, slashing all the way.

Call it Planet Barnevik.

The hard-charging chief executive of Zurich-based ABB Asea Brown Boveri (Holding) Ltd. has seen the future, and it contains no national boundaries. That's why the driven Swede has used more than 60 acquisitions on five continents in just five years to set up a constellation of factories stretching from Stamford to Sydney that would serve a customer base reaching from Kingston to Kuala Lumpur. Put simply, Percy Barnevik wants to sell power equipment to the world. All of it. Everywhere.

This is a global company with a difference, however. Barnevik wants his giant, with annual revenues of $32 billion, to capitalize on local differences but to fear no borders. To do that, he is relying on a human element that knows no nationality: the spirit of enterprise. He is ripping down bureaucracy so executives in

Atlanta can launch new products without meddling from head-quarters, so power technicians in Sweden can make design changes, and so factory workers in India can alter production methods on their own. "I now have an army of 25,000 in profit-center teams," says Barnevik. If you can really build a small-business atmosphere, "you don't have to push or entice managers every day. It becomes a self-motivated force."

Barnevik's brand of corporate shock treatment is certainly not for the faint of heart. The ABB chief and his management trou-bleshooters love to use the R-word—revolution—as their battle cry. They quickly slash administrative staff at acquisitions by up to 90%. And they don't shrink from savaging an existing corpo-rate culture. "You need a big chemical reaction to change a com-pany operating with an outdated view of the world," argues Eberhard von Koerber, ABB's European regional director.

Von Koerber knows a thing or two about strong reactions. He was burned in effigy by workers protesting ABB's radical restructuring of the former Brown Boveri after it merged with Barnevik's Asea in 1987. Not that the protests slowed him down. "The important thing is to judge how much you can rock the boat without sinking it," he says.

While breaking down the old structure is critical, it's just the start. The real secret of Barnevik's success is his ability, after clearing the debris from his tear-down-the-house policies, to motivate remaining managers to stretch themselves to the limit day in and day out—as entrepreneurs do.

Just ask Joachim Schneider. A Brown Boveri factory manager when it merged with Asea to create ABB, he feared the loss of the traditional Swiss-German culture. "We were all more or less functionaries," recalls Schneider, who was used to telling top management each year that his plant simply couldn't produce a profit.

Suddenly, Schneider found himself running a profit center. His success—or failure—was now tied to that of his plant, which built high-voltage power stations. That brought the point home. "It became clear to me that I personally had to push change down through the ranks," he says.

Results weren't long in coming. Schneider visited factories in Sweden that Barnevik already had humming at double or triple the efficiency of similar German plants. He aped those changes back home and was astonished when profits took off in 1989. Two years later, Schneider reorganized his $200 million profit center, creating dozens of new mini centers by line of business instead of function. "Product units developed an unbelievable dynamic which I had never seen before," he says.

Even in near-hopeless cases Schneider found magic. His instinct last year was to kill a line of power-plant components that were getting slammed by low-cost competition from Poland. But he decided to at least try making even this money-loser a profit center and delegated management to a 35-year-old executive. The manager quickly discovered his competitive advantage. "He delivered faster than the Poles, so he could demand a higher price," says Schneider. The $40 million unit is now one of Schneider's most profitable businesses. "No top manager could have seen that advantage—they were too far removed from the market," he says.

Key to the success of Barnevik's strategy has been breaking ABB into 5,000 profit centers, each an autonomous business unit responsible for its own profitability and held accountable for its own failure. His guiding principles are the lessons learned from earlier decentralizations at Asea and steelmaker Sandvik. He similarly restructured the merged Asea-Brown Boveri, creating some 1,300 companies with some having as few as 10 employees. "We went overboard in a couple of cases," he admits, "but it's better to go too far than to compromise up front." When it comes to shaking up a big company, he figures, "you can practically never do too much at one time."

Case in point: The old Brown Boveri operations in Germany. Brown Boveri managers initially begged to phase the changes in with three stages over six years, rather than two years. They said that in Germany such radical moves would be impossible and that ABB would have to adapt to the German management culture. "They said: 'You're going to destroy us,'" recalls von Koerber. "I had to hear it every day."

Top ABB executives were not a sympathetic audience. They felt one small cutback after another would be even more demoralizing than restructuring in one fell swoop. A staggered series of cuts also can impair management's credibility. Most important, they figured gradual restructuring would lose critical momentum as opponents gathered strength.

And the opponents were already plenty strong. German management, local politicians, religious leaders, and workers called repeatedly for von Koerber's dismissal. Unions staunchly opposed the proposed cuts of 4,000 people, or 10% of workers. Opponents ridiculed the new "American management style" that focused only on profits.

But von Koerber wouldn't budge, because the very credibility of the merger was at stake. Not only was the largest of the merged company's subsidiaries in Germany, but both he and Barnevik feared that Swedish and Swiss managers would launch similar campaigns if they saw the German resistance prevail. "Many hoped it wouldn't work out so they could hide behind it," says von Koerber.

After six months of diplomatically presenting the economic rationale for restructuring Brown Boveri, ABB decided to play hardball. Von Koerber told German union leaders that if they continued to resist change, ABB would be forced to transfer work from factories in Germany to more competitive countries. A compromise was then worked out with union leaders on job cuts—2,500 instead of 4,000—but only on the condition that productivity would rise sharply at factories spared from closing.

But the controversy surrounding his early cuts obscured the crucial incentives at the core of his strategy. Barnevik also enforces three laws at merged companies to encourage personal initiative: Managers can make decisions fast and be right; they can make decisions fast and occasionally be wrong; they cannot make decisions slowly.

That approach has struck a chord with many ABB managers. "My boss lets me run my own business. That's what ABB is about," says Nicolas Stroud, a 20-year Westinghouse Electric Corp. veteran who always dreamed of having his own company. He finally got the chance when ABB bought Westinghouse in 1989. Stroud put his Greensburg (Pa.) power-circuit plant back in the black within a year, and doubled sales to $105 million in three years. He didn't see the tough new goals instituted by Barnevik as unreasonable. "Unless you set stretch goals, you won't be competitive," he says. "You don't make all of them, but if you challenge yourself, you make a lot."

One of Barnevik's potent weapons for creating converts is bringing skeptical managers to see ABB in action. He typically gets one factory running at peak efficiency and then shuttles in managers from less-profitable units across the world to see it. "You have to exploit your success stories to break resistance," explains Barnevik. "We human beings are driven by habit, history, and the rear-view mirror. If you want to break direction, you have to shake people up, not by threatening them, not by offering a bonus, but by illustrating in a similar situation what can be accomplished."

That climate encourages employees to break the mold and innovate. For instance, to force administrative personnel to solve problems faster at the rotor factory in Birr, Switzerland, Armin Meyer, president of ABB's Power Generation unit, moved an entire floor of administrators out of their separate office building into the noisy factory. Disoriented and angry at first, the white-collar staff gradually saw the virtue of the change. Factory workers no longer had to trek over to the office building to report such problems as machine breakdowns. Now, silence in the factory provides eloquent notice to the administrators that a problem needs attention. "It was my idea to have the office in the factory 15 years ago," says factory manager Friedrich Mez. "Back then, I was told it couldn't be done. Workers should work, not talk."

Talking, rather than complex strategizing, is what Barnevik's management method is all about. And at ABB, the talking occurs at all levels, inside each factory and between managers and workers half a world apart. Each profit-center chief regularly reveals his financial and operating performance numbers at huge meetings of several hundred middle managers. The middle managers then are responsible for sharing that data—both good and bad—with ABB's tens of thousands of workers worldwide.

Giving workers access to performance figures gets competitive juices flowing. But Barnevik takes it one step further, using internal benchmarking as a tool to relentlessly boost productivity. Monthly performance rankings at ABB's 50 transformer plants, for example, put managers in the hot seat if they are not near the top of the list. "The absolute overriding successful thing is cases, cases, cases," insists Barnevik. "We don't wonder how a competitor does it. The competitor is inside [ABB]. We can go and look at his books."

Barnevik's latest experiment is pushing decentralization down to the factory floor in Sweden, breaking up old work patterns, and promoting continuous learning and teamwork without formal supervision. He hopes to delegate more and more autonomy within each small work group, widening responsibility and rotating jobs to foster versatility. "What we are seeing there in release of human power is unbelievable," says Barnevik. He notes that sick leave, which once ranged up to 25% of the work force, has dropped to just 4%.

The whirlwind of change set off by Barnevik has yet to produce the financial results he wants. Profits plunged 17% last year, to $505 million, as the recessions that have rolled through economies around the world have taken their toll. As a result, Barnevik's goals of a 25% return on capital and 10% operating margins are far from the current 18% and 7%, respectively.

Stock analysts are confident ABB is well positioned for a pickup in world economic growth, however. "When volume comes back, operating profits must explode," says Thomas Pfyl of Bank Vontobel in Zurich. Kevin Brau, analyst at Credit Suisse First Boston in London, estimates Barnevik will hit his operating-margin goal by 1996.

Don't expect the ever-impatient Barnevik to take any comfort from projections. In late August he announced another major restructuring of the company, dividing it into three regions covering the Americas, Europe, and Asia. He charged off $500 million to close 15 more factories. And he says he will continue trimming about 1,000 staffers a month from ABB's 218,000 payroll.

His plans involve more than cutting. He's continuing to buy businesses in Eastern Europe, with a goal of $1.5 billion in sales there by 1995. And Barnevik is spending $1 billion over five years to expand in Asia, where he hopes to get a third of ABB sales by the year 2000.

To Barnevik, problems and challenges are only the catalysts for improvement. "You can get enormous change when you are forced to redesign your processes all the time," he says. "You constantly have new targets, new targets, new targets." In his world, the revolution never stops.

By Gail E. Schares

14

Jack Welch on the Art of Thinking Small

"Speed is really the driver that everyone is after."

Few chief executives understand the challenge of fostering enterprise within a mammoth corporation more than General Electric Co. Chairman John F. Welch Jr. Since he became CEO in 1981, he has transformed GE from a plodding, bureaucracy-laden giant into a lean, sharply focused paradigm of contemporary management. Welch discussed his philosophy with Business Week's *Connecticut Bureau Manager Tim Smart and Senior Editor Judith H. Dobrzynski.*

Why is there such a fascination with small companies? What are you learning from them?

Speed is really the driver that everyone is after. Faster products, faster product cycles to market. Better response time to customers. And there's no question that the smaller one is, and the easier the communication is, the faster one gets. The customer is a much more real person to you, because the customer in a very small company determines what you're going to eat next week. Satisfying customers, getting faster communications, moving with more agility, all these things are easier when one is small. And these are all the characteristics one needs in a fast-moving global environment.

Do you visit with these companies?

I came from a small company. I came from (GE's) plastics company. It was very small, and we ran it like a family grocery store. I would argue that we run GE in a very informal manner. It allows you to get rid of all the ritual and the rigmarole that ties up companies.

Is there a GE business now that is analogous to a small company?

GE Capital has a myriad of activities that replicate that today. I think that our plastics business today is fast-moving and very entrepreneurial. And I think every one of our businesses is infinitely faster than it used to be.

What kinds of businesses within GE moved first?

You normally associate productivity with high growth, rapid technology change, new business. Well, the business that broke the productivity code in GE was lighting. A hundred years old, 2% a year growth. But they got a mindset around productivity. So they began that launch. And quick response, the ability to get inventory turns very rapidly, that came out of appliances. Not an exciting, fast-moving, revolutionary business. GE Capital clearly has seeded more new businesses of late than anybody else.

Do you bring in small-business people for advisory sessions?

We had Marvin Mann [of IBM spin-off Lexmark]. He came to talk about life in a small company that used to be a division of a big company. And the differences of Lexmark by itself vs. Lexmark in IBM. But I think we all know what we want out of a small company. We know the characteristics: informality, lack of layers, getting close to the customers, making everybody's actions feel like they're important so they [consider] the implications of their actions. Small companies all understand that.

How would you rate the Japanese in terms of flexibility and speed and getting close to the customer?

They're battling a currency issue, but they have the same wonderful characteristics they had when everyone was praising them. They are still fast. They are still very team-oriented. They really do try to meet customer needs. Their quality is first-rate.

Yet they do it in a different way. They're more hierarchical, aren't they?

[Japanese managers] set out the objective, but the [low-level] people do a lot of the figuring out of how to get the thing done. The problem that we had as a country, I think, was that our management gave people the command and then told them exactly how to do it. Now, once you tell everybody how to do it, they might as well not have a brain.

It seems that within our corporate culture, some people who rise to the top might have trouble not giving specific directions, and adapting to this new kind of management.

Don't get me [wrong]. This is not a rudderless ship that we're talking about. The objectives are clearly in focus. We still want to be No. 1 and No. 2 in every business we're in on a global basis. Or we don't want to be in it. So everyone clearly has a focus on what they're doing....It isn't: "Let's come in and have a party here." It's: "Let's gain share, let's get productivity, let's be sure we globalize."

Is there a size or development stage when a small company loses its edge?

As a small company expands rapidly, it runs the risk of setting up structures to manage its growth. And it is the trickiest thing in the world to keep a small company on a growth trajectory and maintain the atmosphere that got them to the dance.

What lessons have you learned that they would benefit from knowing about?

Managers tend, in the growth cycle, to question in great depth businesses that are in trouble, but to not question those delivering the goods. [Harvard business school professor] John Kotter, he's got a beautiful diagram. He talks about what happens in high-growth situations and what the organization does. The people start to believe that they are the reasons for the high growth. Then, they organize to manage the high growth. They put in all the bureaucracy, and the bureaucracies start feeding on each other. The customer then gets further and further pushed away.

We have seen any number of companies go up the curve and come down it. Power systems in the early '80s, aircraft engines now. And I take this little thing of Kotter's and every time somebody's behaving this way, I write 'em a little note. And I send this out to them.

Does it then require a different type of manager in the process?

It is very difficult—not impossible, but very difficult—for

people who have experienced 10% to 15% to 20%-a-year growth for several years to come to the reality of a changing environment. Now, we've had some successes with this, the most notable one being a locomotive business some years ago where the team did all this and then changed the tires, as we say, while the car was running, because they had to.

Some companies, such as Xerox, have technology ventures where little seedlings bloom. Is there anywhere in GE where you develop really small businesses?

We feel that we can grow within a business, but we are not interested in incubating new businesses. We made a clear, conscious decision—to be argued by some people—that we do not run this incubation laboratory off by itself.

Small-business people say that when they're first starting a business, all of their energy goes into product development or the technology. But then the business gets to a certain size and they complain that all they do is worry about personnel or financing. And they get away from the things they did to get the business started.

That's all we are: personnel directors. But we [headquarters managers] accept that role. If we get the right people in the right job, we've won the game. We spend days and days on assessments of people, interviewing people, talking to people. Picking out stock-option recipients. We're dealing with money to allocate to projects and people to allocate to businesses. And we don't do any product development, any pricing, anything like that.

I think you gotta know what your job is. And our jobs aren't picking colors for refrigerators or designing crisper trays.

You're fascinated with Sam Walton?

Yeah.

What has GE learned from Wal-Mart? It's not a small business, but—

It behaves like one, and it's entrepreneurial. Wal-Mart, in my opinion, clearly made a connection between the customer and every employee in Wal-Mart. And they work on that every single day. They just can't stand not filling a customer need. If they're out of blankets in Minneapolis, they've got a computer system that will move the blankets instantaneously to Minneapolis. Or their antifreeze is low in Chicago and high in Kalamazoo, they'll move it. An insatiable desire to make customers love 'em. And tying their personal rewards over the years to doing that, they've seen enormous wealth created at all levels of the store.

We have copied that through QMI, quick market intelligence, in various forms. Our medical business, for example. People say, well, you can't do that in a medical business—heavy equipment, magnetic resonance machines, and stuff like that. But every Friday, their QMI session is aimed at medical today. "Tell us what you need to get that installation in next week." And everybody is on the phone. The plant manager, the engineering manager, all the head guys. That's our adaptation of a Wal-Mart thing.

So what happens when that field person says: "I need a cat scanner or an X-ray machine at St. Vincent's Hospital?"

We'll get it there.

What's the chain of things that happens?

The plant then has to get back [and change] their assignment. The manufacturing manager is sitting there. And if there's an installation at Mt. Sinai [Hospital] that doesn't need to be installed that fast, they'll move it to St. Vincent's and fill in Mt. Sinai two weeks later.

You mentioned expanding the reward system from 300 to 14,000 employees?

No, about 8,000, 9,000, something like that.

And that's stock options?

Yes.

That is one of the ways small companies energize their employees.

You should see the pulse of this place when the stock hits 100. The building almost shakes. Because lots of people, at all levels, have options.

How do you decide to give someone a stock option?

Some people believe in giving broad stock options to all employees. We like to differentiate. We have all kinds of guidelines. [For example,] 50 percent of them have to be less than 10 years in the company. To mix it up. So that people aren't just handing it out as a routine thing.

Another small-company thing here is I meet once a quarter with all the purchasing people. And they're all in telling their vignettes about what they're doing, too. We meet with all the sales managers once a quarter. So they're sharing best practices.

So doing that, we end up being right down in the trenches on a lot of details. That's a small-company attribute, I think.

There's a flip side to it, though. There are a lot of small-business people worrying about whether their payroll checks are going to bounce who would love to have GE's financial muscle. So bigness gives you something.

We can stay in businesses that other people had to leave because they couldn't hang in there. Your training skills and strengths are bigger and better. But the thing that we're all trying to do—and I don't think GE's any different than anybody else—we're desperately trying to combine the best of both.

Is the government heading in the right direction?

Much of the job creation in small companies has come from the desire of big companies to do what they do best and let small companies do what they do best. Big companies are the engine for small companies. The idea that a government is off creating these small things and then they're going to do [big] things is a form of kidding themselves.

GE people spend a lot of time going to suppliers....

Working with 'em?

Some would say putting pressure on them. But it's making them move quicker or sell faster or whatever.

I'm not embarrassed to say: "Put pressure on them." I'm not timid about that. All these small companies that serve us, the machine shops around all of our plants, are gone if we lose the competitive business. If we go out of the turbine business in Schenectady, [it's] lights out for all the entrepreneurs that have done so wonderfully serving us.

What about the trend toward breaking up? IBM is the company that people think of, but other companies feel the only way they can get a small soul is to chop up all the parts.

I don't buy that. I think the opportunity for big companies is to create, to take advantage of what size brings them. And create within that framework the speed, the informality, and the things you need, the customer contact, of a small company. If the only way you can get small feelings is to blow it up, what's the role of management? Because being big and agile is better than being small and agile. The only reason people are small is they can't get big. Nobody wants to stay small. The objective is to grow.

15

Women Entrepreneurs: They're Forming Small Businesses at Twice the Rate of Men

In 1989 Fran Greene was "female and facing 50, which is death in Corporate America," she recalls. So after 25 years with a big electronics-components supplier, Greene struck out on her own and started Sun State Electronics, a Winter Springs (Fla.) distribution company that sells high-tech gear to the aerospace and defense industries. Today, it's a $2.5 million business that employs 10 people. At 52, Greene, a former sales representative, has branched out into a second venture: Cakes Across America, which contracts with bakeries nationwide to deliver cakes for all occasions.

Gianna "Gigi" Dekko Goldman gave in to her entrepreneurial longings in 1990, quitting her marketing job at Minnetonka Inc.'s Claire Burke fragrances to start a business selling picture frames. Today, Gianna International in Rowayton, Conn., has more than $1 million in sales. A big plus to being her own boss is having a flexible lifestyle, reflects Goldman, 34. "I wanted to continue my career in an aggressive way, but I also wanted to be a mom."

Economic necessity drove Nancy Novinc, 42, and Hillary Sterba, 49, to start their tool-engineering company two years ago. They had just been laid off from Cleveland Twist Drill Co., a manufacturer of cutting tools, when they decided to start S&N Engineering Services Corp. "We decided if we were going to put in these long hours and work this hard, we would do it for ourselves," observes Sterba.

Different women, different dreams, and very different businesses. But they're all part of a wave of women entrepreneurs who are reshaping the American small-business landscape. While women have long owned businesses or toiled behind the scenes in family companies, their numbers are reaching giant proportions in the small-business sector—one of the most dynamic parts of the U.S. economy. There are roughly 6.5 million enterprises with fewer than 500 employees that are owned or controlled by women in the U.S. That's almost a third of the total, according to estimates by the National Foundation for Women Business Owners (NFWBO). Already, one in ten American workers is employed by a woman-owned company.

And the ranks of such companies are growing: Women are forming small businesses at nearly twice the rate of their male counterparts. "It's a combination of women being more educated, feeling more entitled, wanting to combine lives and careers, and seeing that [business ownership] is where most growth and opportunities are," says Lynda L. Moore, professor of management at Simmons College in Boston.

Talent Pool. The phenomenon isn't limited to services and neighborhood retail shops—the traditional preserves of women who wanted to be their own bosses. True, most women entrepreneurs are drawn to the retail and services trades in part because of low startup costs. But the advances of female executives throughout Corporate America have produced a new pool of talent with experience in many industries. Now, as they leave large companies to strike out on their own, women are often starting businesses in such longtime male bastions as manufacturing and construction,. For example, Novinc, former director of new products at Cleveland Twist Drill, and Sterba, once the manager of national account services, together had 26 years of experience in the industrial-tool business when they began their company.

The impact of women's entrepreneurship is also resonating far beyond the confines of small business. Many experts believe that women business owners often seem to emphasize employee training, teamwork, reduced hierarchy, and quality far more than their male counterparts. As a result, they may offer distinctive lessons in management styles that are now being embraced by Corporate America as it strives to improve its global competitiveness. "Women tend to be more cooperative, informal, consensus-building in their behavior," says Candida G. Brush, assistant professor of management policy at Boston University, who recently reviewed 200 studies on male and female management styles. Men, in contrast, "tend to approach things in a more competitive, formal, or systematic way," adds Brush. Goldman puts it more simply: "Women have been taught all their lives to nurture and support others. As entrepreneurs, we are really able to use our natural abilities to empower others in our own companies."

"What's more, women tend to measure success differently. While they care about profits, they believe their ultimate success rests on the development of their employees and on exceeding customer expectations, says Nancy C. Pechloff, director of the Enterprise Group at Arthur Andersen & Co. "Women are likely to spend more money on training and developing their people because they think that's going to give them a competitive advantage," she explains.

Marilyn Burns's business sums up the female style of management. Burns has stressed employee development almost from the day she founded Marilyn Burns Education Associates in 1984 to help teachers teach math better. To share ideas with her 17 employees and 65 independent consultants, Burns installed an electronic bulletin board. Her office staffers in Sausalito, Calif., attend two day-long retreats each year and are encouraged to take seminars and classes to improve everything from writing to computer skills. A "staff development committee" creates in-house training programs, and a "barometer committee" handles gripes and suggestions at the $2.4 million company. "It has to be a learning environment," says Burns.

Sensitive.   The female management approach is being felt by the employees of women-owned businesses. Economists have long debated the quality of jobs created by small businesses, which often offer lower pay and fewer benefits than big corporations. But a study soon to be released by the NFWBO finds that women-owned companies, while likely to provide the same basic benefits as all small companies, are more likely to offer tuition reimbursement and flextime. Moreover, women business owners are more likely to offer profit-sharing for employees at an earlier stage in the life of the company.

Gun Denhart, for one, says she's sensitive to her workers' needs. The CEO of Hanna Andersson in Portland, Ore., a $43 million cataloger that sells children's clothing, pays for half of her employees' child-care costs, up to $3000 a year. "We definitely have other goals than just the bottom line," says Denhart.

In addition to a more worker-friendly environment, companies run by women entrepreneurs may offer a more secure job than the typical small business. Paradoxically, that may be because women's businesses don't grow as fast as men's do. Some blame outright discrimination or a lack of access to capital for the slower expansion. But small-business consultant David L. Birch, president of Cognetics Inc., speculates that many women are reining in growth because of concerns about quality, customer service, and employees. In a study of women-owned companies that Birch completed in 1992 for the NFWBO, he found that women's companies were twice as likely as all companies to be stable or slow-growing. And that, in turn, may mean that it's safer to work for a woman-owned company: About 15% of the women-owned businesses showed job losses, compared with 23% of all businesses, says Birch.

Consider Sue Carroll, owner of Country Garden Inc., which produces hair accessories and bridal pieces. Her 16-year-old company employs 20 people in Kirkland, Wash., and has about $1 million in sales. Carroll is not against making money. But she believes the demands of a bigger company wouldn't allow her to change her product lines quickly enough to suit her customers. "We would lose some of the freedom we have now if we grow much more," says Carroll.

Hurdles.   As their companies multiply, women entrepreneurs are gaining more clout. Often excluded from the old boy networks, women are forming their own groups to swap management ideas and customer leads. Since 1991, the National Association of Women Business Owners has seen its membership rise 38%, to 4700. And grass-roots efforts are blossoming, too.

Despite their gains, women entrepreneurs still face huge obstacles. Although there has been some progress on the financing front, they still have problems raising money. Lacking access to many traditional credit sources, 52% of women business owners used credit cards for short-term financing during 1992, according to a survey by the NFWBO. That compares with only 18% for all small-to-midsize companies. And women have lagged in grabbing their share of business. Data from 1987, the latest available, show women-owned businesses, which then accounted for 27% of all companies, with only 4.5% of all business receipts. Women also get only 1.5% of the $200 billion spent by Washington to purchase goods and services.

Whatever the hurdles, there's plenty of fuel to keep this entrepreneurial fire burning. The downsizing of Corporate America, the so-called glass ceiling that blocks women from top jobs, and a desire to balance work and family are among the driving forces. "Women are finding it's time to own the system and not just ask permission to join it," says Joline Godfrey, founder of An Income of Her Own, a national program that introduces teenage girls to entrepreneurship.

Goldman came to a similar conclusion when she started Gianna International. She had spent three years as a product manager at General Mills Inc. but felt her career prospects were limited. When she saw no women on the executive roster, she says: "I knew that could hurt me." Goldman also wanted to start a family eventually, but she feared kids would land her on the Mommy Track, stunting her career prospects further. Those concerns persisted when she later went to work for Minnetonka. "My feeling is that a boss and a baby don't mix," she says. Today, Goldman sells stylish photograph frames to such powerhouse retailers as Dayton Hudson Corp. and Saks Fifth Avenue. She's hoping that her business will soon have enough momentum to allow her to start planning a family.

Some women are drawn to small business because they believe they can accomplish far more professionally by running their own enterprise. "In the corporate environment, there are so many limitations placed on you," says Deborah L. Hueppeler, a Wharton School MBA who left Merrill Lynch Private Capital in Dallas and bought a chain of 28 brake-repair shops in 1990 with a local investor's aid. She plans to expand the $10 million Just Brakes Corp. to 200 shops within five years.

Still, entrepreneurship can be an especially risky and daunting effort for women. Women entrepreneurs typically start out with far less capital than their male counterparts. A recent Marquette University study of Wisconsin entrepreneurs found that women had a median startup amount of $15,000 for a one-women company, compared with $36,000 for male entrepreneurs. That may be because women often start service businesses that need less capital or because they have fewer assets for collateral. And their personal networks may fall short. "Men still tend to belong to organizations where a handshake and a referral will get them the money they need to get started," says Wendy Reid-Crisp, national director of the National Association for Female Executives.

Customer Chase.   Some experts also believe that many women are simply more cautious in their borrowing, more easily intimidated by lenders, and less informed about financing sources. Cynthia L. Iannarelli, director of the National Education Center for Women in Business at Seton Hill College in Greensburg, Pa., also says that it doesn't help that most bankers and accountants are men, many of whom "still have these stereotypical ideas about what women can do."

Rochelle Zabarkes certainly wishes she had started out with more capital when she opened a specialty food store on Manhattan's trendy Upper West Side in 1991 after 20 years as a video producer. At first, she scraped together funds from friends, family, and business contacts. With $50,000 in hand, she then turned to the Manhattan Borough Development Corp. and the National Association for Female Executives, raising an additional $210,000. Still, the financial cushion proved too thin when customer traffic fell off during the recent recession. "If I had to do it over again, I would ask for $1 million," says Zabarkes, who has kept Adriana's Bazaar afloat only after losing her home, filing for personal bankruptcy, and placing her company in Chapter 11. She expects she will finally break even this year—just as the landlord is threatening to evict her over $50,000 in unpaid rent.

Even women who own thriving businesses often have a hard time obtaining capital to grow. When she needed $3 million for expansion last year, Paula George Tompkins didn't go to any bank. Instead, she sought funding from a half-dozen venture-capital firms so her company, SoftAd Group, could introduce new interactive-marketing software and services. Even with a nine-year record and sales of about $5 million for her Mill Valley (Calif.) company, Tompkins was turned down.

It didn't help that her business was a labor-intensive service company, she admits. But she also believes the refusals had a lot to do with her gender. "I'm young. I'm a woman. I just don't think they took me very seriously," she says. So Tompkins, 41, "boot-strapped" the expansion with internal funds and overtime from her employees. Still, she says she lost a year in the marketplace with her new products.

Drumming up customers can be just as challenging as chasing capital. Many women still find themselves on the outs when it comes to male-dominated business networks, a convenient method of scoping out prospective clients. Novinc and Sterba, for instance, say they were denied membership in a local Cleveland trade association because they supposedly didn't fit the criteria in the bylaws. "No one ever showed us the bylaws," says Sterba. That hasn't stopped the pair. They have called on customers and colleagues they had dealt with at their previous jobs, who offered advice on everything from products to leads on customers. "We're both very aggressive individuals," says Sterba.

Minority women can feel even more frozen out. Just ask Ella D. Williams, an African-American and owner of Aegir Systems Inc. in Oxnard, Calif., an engineering and consulting company.

Despite 13 years with Hughes Electronics as a systems analyst, Williams had a tough time landing her first contract when she struck out on her own in 1981. "There's a general negativity about doing business with minorities, as if we didn't know anything," she says. "Prejudice is part of business. You have to deal with it and can't dwell on it, or it overwhelms you." To reach potential clients, she says, she followed her mother's advice about getting to a man's heart. "I started making cheesecakes, breads, and muffins and took them on sales calls. I still do that today," says Williams, 53.

Perhaps the one dream women entrepreneurs relinquish is the notion that they'll have more time for themselves and their families. Wendy Wilson left her job as head of investor relations at AMR Corp., parent of American Airlines Inc., after five years of working 14-hour days and weekends because "I wanted to have a life." Now, she's working even longer hours at her own investor-relations company. And she often has trouble sleeping. But, she says, "I'm much happier because I'm in control of it."

As more women take control of their economic destinies, Wilson isn't the only one staying awake nights. And with their growing visibility and clout, Wilson and other women entrepreneurs may soon feel comfortable ignoring their mothers when they ask: "Have you thought about getting a real job?"

By Wendy Zellner, with Resa W. King,
Veronica N. Byrd, Gail DeGeorge, and Jane Birnbaum

16

Business Week/ Harris Executive Poll: What's Worrying Small Business

Think availability of credit is the biggest problem facing small business? Guess again: The owners and managers of small companies say it's a distant fourth on their list of woes, behind healthcare costs, government regulations, and staffing. That was just one of the findings of a 1993 poll of more than 400 owners of small companies. Here are some of the results.

Trouble Spots

- How serious a problem for your business is each of the following?

	Very serious	Some-what serious	Not very serious	Not serious at all	Not sure
The cost of health insurance for your employees	58%	25%	7%	9%	1%
Government regulations	45%	31%	13%	11%	0%
Finding and keeping qualified employees	23%	20%	26%	21%	0%
Difficulty in obtaining financing	17%	26%	22%	32%	3%
Litigation	15%	26%	27%	30%	2%

Key Concerns

- Which one of these is the most serious problem for your company?

The cost of health insurance for your employees	34%	Difficulty in obtaining financing	12%
Government regulations	30%	Litigation	2%
Finding and keeping qualified employees	20%	Not sure	2%

Money Sources

- Where does most of your working capital come from now?

Bank loans	34%	Federal or state government funding	3%
Funds generated from operations	33%	Public stock offerings	2%
Family, friends, or private investors	17%	Factors or other finance companies	2%
Grants and contributions	2%	Credit cards	1%
Venture capitalists	1%	Other sources	2%
		Not sure	3%

Fishing for Funds...

- Have you sought to get financing from banks or other sources in the last six months, or not?

Yes	36%
No	63%
Not sure	1%

...And Reeling Them In

- If yes: Did you get all the financing you needed, most of it, only some of it, or none of it? (144 responding)

All	55%
Most of it	14%
Only some	13%
None	16%
Not sure	2%

Outward Bound

- Does your company export goods or services to any other country?

Yes	18%
No	82%
Not sure	0%

Job Histories

- Before you worked for this company, did you work for a much larger company, a somewhat larger company, a similar-sized company, a somewhat smaller company, or a much smaller company?

Much larger	34%	Much smaller	11%
Somewhat larger	9%	Only worked for this company	17%
Similar size	13%	Not sure	2%
Somewhat smaller	14%		

Survey of 401 owners and managers of companies with 6 to 500 employees conducted March 16–31, 1993, for *Business Week* by Louis Harris & Associates Inc.

Edited by Mark N. Vamos

17

Self Test: How Entrepreneurial Is Your Company?

The essence of an entrepreneurial company has little to do with size. The secret lies more in the company's mind-set than in its balance sheet, cash flow, technology, or other factors. How a company prepares for, engages in, and pursues its battles for the marketplace is what counts most.

The following quiz was prepared by Professor Jeffry A. Timmons of Babson College and Harvard business school, where he is the MBA Class of 1954 Professor of New Ventures. The quiz yields clues to the complicated entrepreneurial genetic code of management philosophy, strategies, practices, and culture. Except for statement #2, note your response as follows: strongly agree (SA), inclined to agree (IA), inclined to disagree (ID), and strongly disagree (SD). While in some cases the "entrepreneurial" response may seem obvious, the only way to get an honest appraisal of your company is to select the most accurate response that most closely approximates your situation. For scoring, see page 114.

1. The main things that determine how people get ahead at my company are the size of my budget and the number of people who report to me.

2. Our goal is to generate the following proportion of sales from products introduced in the past five years: a) 50% or more; b) 40%–50%; c) 20%–30%; d) 10%–20%; e) less than 10%; f) no goal.

3. The best new product or service ideas we have come from within the company, mainly from R&D or marketing research people.

4. Our company is so big now that it isn't worth our while getting into a small or poorly defined market. We aren't very interested in new projects that require a commitment of less than $5 million in capital.

5. Two of our top people want to launch a new business that they would own and manage. It has a good chance of succeeding. They want our company to provide financial and strategic support—even a minority investment. They also want salaries and stock options pegged to the new business' results. Their proposal would stand a good chance of being approved.

6. A manager wants to leave to start her own business. We would do whatever we can to prevent her departure, including strict enforcement of a noncompete agreement.

7. A manager at my company has had to shut down a business for which he had been an enthusiastic champion. The losses are not huge by company standards. The manager can count on the silent treatment from colleagues, and an unappealing new assignment.

8. If I were running my company, I would immediately begin to change many of its policies and procedures, including budgeting, hiring, and rewarding people.

9. At my company, people at every level, down to the production line and maintenance, have a clear understanding of how their jobs and daily decisions affect the company's financial performance.

10. My company is highly committed to the strategic process. In deciding what new businesses to get into, we involve the board and top management from the beginning to make sure we have it right before we launch a venture.

11. We don't give up easily. Once we commit our company to a strategy, we allocate a lot of capital and people and pursue it with a vengeance.

12. Our strategic process begins by identifying opportunities. Then we figure out which ones offer the most sustainable growth and fit with who we are and what we want to become. We abandon initiatives fairly quickly if we aren't getting the results we want.

13. Because of a strategic shift, our company has decided to sell a small but successful division for a hefty profit. The top managers who have been running the division for years have decided to stay with our company. We would reward their effort by paying them a bonus equivalent to 10% of the gain, even if that amounted to millions of dollars.

14. Pursuing new business opportunities is a priority around here. But we're so busy with day-to-day operations that we usually think about new ventures only in our spare time or in occasional idea meetings.

15. My company has what could be called a "perpetual learning" culture. We are so committed that we will go to the extreme of reimbursing people for any educational expenses, job-related or not.

SCORING THE ENTREPRENEURIAL COMPANY QUIZ

The statements on this and the previous page focus on five facets of an entrepreneurial mindset: resources, opportunities, incentives, empowerment, and strategy. Add up your point score (see next page) using the following symbols (except question #2): SA = strongly agree; IA = inclined to agree; ID = inclined to disagree; SD = strongly disagree.

Score your response to each item as

1.	SD(4)	ID(3)	IA(2)	SA(1)	
2.	A(5)	B(4)	C(3)	D(2)	E(1) F(0)
3.	SD(4)	ID(3)	IA(2)	SA(1)	
4.	SD(4)	ID(3)	IA(2)	SA(1)	
5.	SA(4)	IA(3)	ID(2)	SD(1)	
6.	SD(4)	ID(3)	IA(2)	SA(1)	
7.	SD(4)	ID(3)	IA(2)	SA(1)	
8.	SD(4)	ID(4)	IA(2)	SA(1)	
9.	SA(4)	IA(4)	ID(2)	SD(1)	
10.	SD(4)	ID(3)	IA(2)	SA(1)	
11.	SD(4)	ID(3)	IA(2)	SA(1)	
12.	SA(4)	IA(3)	ID(2)	SD(1)	
13.	SA(4)	IA(3)	ID(2)	SD(1)	
14.	SD(4)	ID(3)	IA(2)	SA(1)	
15.	SA(4)	ID(3)	ID(2)	ID(1)	

How Your Company Rates on Key Aspects of an Entrepreneurial Mind-Set

High scores on the following groups of statements mean you're excelling in those areas:

Resources (#1, #4, #5).   Your company knows how to gain access to resources. It doesn't worry about owning or maximizing resources. It concentrates on getting the resources it needs and putting them to their best use.

Opportunities (#2, #3, #14).   Your company fosters an opportunity-driven process. Regardless of the resources it owns or controls, it appreciates that the best ideas and opportunities come from customers, rather than from within the company.

Incentives (#6, #7, #13).   Your company rewards action and calculated risk-taking by basing incentives on long-term value creation and marketplace success or failure—not some internal corporate system.

Empowerment (#8, #9, #15).   Your company empowers its people, particularly by fostering teamwork. It treats employees with respect and values their talents. If you strongly agreed with #8, it means you are thinking entrepreneurially, even if your company isn't.

Strategic process (#10, #11, #12). Your company's strategy is a function of opportunity, not ingrained predispositions. It is also flexible: The company can commit quickly to new ideas and just as quickly abandon unsuccessful ones.

Scoring. 45–61, your company either thinks or acts entrepreneurially; 30–44, your company is doing O.K., but it's probably missing some good opportunities; 29 or less, watch out! Bureaucrats are probably running the show.

Index

ABB Asea Brown Boveri (Holding) Ltd., 87–92
Accion, 50
Adrianna's Bazaar, 104–105
Aegir Systems Inc., 105–106
African-American women entrepreneurs, 105–106
Ambiguity, tolerance of, 5
American Airlines Inc., 61–62
An Income of Her Own, 103
Arkansas Enterprise Group (AEG), 49–50
AT&T, 73
AT&T Capital Corp., 45
Axtell, Robert M., 33

Bank financing, 44–45
    obstacles faced by women and, 104–105
Banking industry, 15
Barnevik, Percy, 87–92
Big companies:
    breaking into smaller units, 71–73, 89, 98
    emulation of entrepreneurial spirit, 25–26
    slowness to adapt to change, 15
    technology at, 22–23, 25–26
    thinking small at, 36, 39, 67–74
Blackie, Gerald R., 4
Blake, Norman O., Jr., 56
Bowman, Michael, 57–58
Burns, Marilyn, 101–102
Business experience, 5
Business training, microlender-provided, 50

Bygrave, William D., 5

Cakes Across America, 99
Callaway, Ely, 5
Callaway Golf Co., 5
Capital-gains tax, 47
Carroll, Sue, 102–103
Caterpillar Inc., 63
Catspaw Inc., 9–10
Chile, entrepreneurship in, 77–79
Chrysler Corp., 64
CIT Group Holdings Inc., 45
"Co-location," 26
Competitiveness, partnerships and, 62
Computer industry, 14
Computer software industry, 14–15
Confidence, 6
Consolidated Rail Corp., 22
Consultants, 26–27
Continental Bank Corp., 72
Continental Cablevision Inc., 5
Cook, Scott D., 6–8
Corporation for Enterprise Development (CED), 50
Country Garden, Inc., 102–103
Credit cards as financing mechanism, 103
CSX Corp., 58
Cuba, 11
Cummins Engine Co., 61
Customers:
    getting closer to, 36–38
    satisfaction of, 34
    women's problems in obtaining, 105–106

Cutbacks, management and, 29–34

Dana Corp., 72
Dannon, 40
Data-base marketing, 36–37
Dell, Michael, 14
Dell Computer Corp., 14
DeLuca, Fred, 4
Denhart, Gun, 102
Detroit Center Tool, 24
Downsizing:
    changing management style and,
        55–59
    checklist for, 32
    of Japanese companies, 82–84
    management and, 29–34
    problems created by, 69–70
Drucker, Peter F., 4
Drug industry, partnerships in,
    64–65
DuPont Co., 33

Early-retirement plans in Japan,
    84
Eastern Europe, 17
Economic forces favoring entrepre-
    neurship, 15–16
Egan, Bruce L., 26–27
Eli Lilly & Co., 64–65
Emerging economies, role of entre-
    preneurs in, 17–18
Emerson, 71
Emmer, Mark B., 9–10
Employees:
    empowerment of, 56–59, 73–74
    giving access to performance fig-
        ures, 91
    recruitment and retention of, as
        problem for small businesses,
        108
    training for (see Training)
    trends in number of, 108–109
    of women-owned businesses,
        101–103

Enterprise Florida, 46
Entrepreneurial characteristics, 3–10
Entrepreneurial companies, value of,
    12–14
Entrepreneurship:
    economic trends favoring, 15–16
    growth of, 13–18, 100
    job histories of entrepreneurs and,
        110
    self test for, 111–115
    threats to, 16
    (*See also* Women entrepreneurs)
Ernst & Young, 46
Experience, 5, 110

Finance, 43–51
    bank, 44–45, 104–105
    microlenders and, 50, 51
    nonbank, 45–47, 103
    obstacles faced by women and,
        103–105
    peer-group lending and, 50–51
    as problem for small businesses,
        108, 109
    sources of, 109
Ford Motor Co., 61

General Electric Co., 63–64, 94
    downsizing of, 31, 33
Gianna International, 99–100,
    103–104
Godfrey, Joline, 103
Goldberg, Edward L., 25–26
Goldman, Gianna Dekko, 99–100,
    103–104
Gorog, William, 8–9
Government regulations as problem
    for small businesses, 108
Greene, Fran, 99
Grousbeck, Irving H., 5
Growth:
    of entrepreneurship, 13–18, 100
    of women-owned businesses,
        102–103

Guaranteed Overnight Delivery Inc., 45

Hanna Andersson, 102
Harnischfeger Corp., 74
Harris, Andrew W., 24
Health insurance costs as problem for small businesses, 108
Health Valley Foods, 39–40
Heller Business Credit, 45
Henderson, J. Bronce, III, 24
Hueppler, Deborah L., 104
Hyatt Hotels, 73–74

IBM Japan, 84
Imperial Chemical Industries PLC, 69
Income limits, microlenders and, 51
Informal venture-capitalist networks, 46
International sales, 110
Intuit, 6–8

Jacobs, Sharon, 55–56
Japanese businesses, 81–85
  Jack Welch on, 94–95
Job quality in women-owned businesses, 102–103
Johnson & Johnson, 71–72
Just Brakes Corp., 104

Kaplan, Steven, 15
Kelleher, Herbert D., 69
Knight, Charles F., 71
Koala Tee Custom Sportswear Inc., 24–25

Lands' End Inc., 25
Learning:
  promoting, 92
  (See also Training)

Legislation, 47
Litigation as problem for small businesses, 108
Loans:
  through Small Business Administration, 44–45
  to women, 103–105
  (See also Finance)
Loneman, Kelly J., 24–25

Management:
  changing style of, 55–59
  cutbacks and, 29–34
  motivating, 88–89
  by women entrepreneurs, 101–103
Manco Inc., 37–38
Manpower International, 62
Marilyn Burns Education Associates, 101–102
Marketing, 35–41
  data-base, 36–37
  niche, 40
  by women, 105–106
Matsushita Electric Industrial Co., 84
Merck & Co., 64
Merrill Lynch & Co., 25–26, 45
Microlenders, 50, 51
  challenges faced by, 51
Miller, Gail, 49–50
Minority women entrepreneurs, 105–106
Mistakes, tolerance for, 59
Morton Metalcraft Co., 63
Motivation of managers, 88–89
Motorola, 65
Muzzillo, Gregory P., 4

National Association for Female Executives, 104, 105
National Association of Women Business Owners, 103
Niche marketing, 40

Nippon Telegraph & Telephone
Corp., 84
Nonbank financing, 45–47, 103
Novinc, Nancy, 100, 101, 105
Nucor Corp., 13–14

Organization, 5
Outsourcing as threat to entrepreneurship, 16

Partnerships, 61–65
Passion, 8
Peer-group lending, 50–51
Pepsi-Cola Co., 34
Performance, giving workers access
to figures on, 91
Pizza Hut, 36–37
Platinum Software Corp., 4
Productivity, Japanese, 83
ProForma Inc., 4
Proulx, Tom, 7–8

Quality, women entrepreneurs'
emphasis on, 102–103
Quicken, 7–8

Red Hook Ale Brewery, 9
Regulations as problem for small
businesses, 108
Reno Air Inc., 62
Research and development,
encouraging, 73
Restructuring:
at ABB Asea Brown Boveri
(Holding) Ltd., 87–92
of Japanese companies, 82–84
(*See also* Downsizing)
Retirement, early, in Japan, 84
Ricoh Co., 84
Risk, acceptance of, 5
Roadway Global Air Inc., 67–68
Russia, entrepreneurship in, 75–77

Sales:
international, 110
trends in, 108
Sanyo Electric Co., 81–84
Shipman, Paul, 9
Small Business Administration, loans
through, 44–45
Small Business Capital Enhancement
Act, 47
Small Business Incentive Act of 1993,
47
Small Business Loan Securitization
and Secondary Market
Enhancement Act, 47
Small businesses:
concerns of, 107–110
performance of, 70
role in United States, 12–14
success versus failure of, 16
technology and, 23—25
women-owned, 99–106
S&N Engineering Services Corp.,
100
SoftAd Group, 105
Software industry, 14–15
Soho Beverages Inc., 40
Southwest Airlines Inc., 69
Span of control, cutbacks and, 31
Speed, Jack Welch on, 93–94
Spiegel, 37
Staff development (*see* Training)
Startup financing, 46
State financial aid, 46
Steel industry, 13–14
Sterba, Hillary, 100, 101, 105
Stock options, Jack Welch on, 97–98
Sun Microsystems, 72
Sun State Electronics, 99

Talking, restructuring and, 91
Tax laws, 47
Teamwork, promoting, 92
Technology, 21–27
at big companies, 22–23, 25–26
at small companies, 23—25

Telemorphix Inc., 24
Tichy, Noel M., 56–57
Tompkins, Paula George, 105
Training:
  emphasis on, by women entrepre-
    neurs, 101–102
  for management, 58
  microlender-provided, 50
Transmedia Inc., 15

U.S. Order, 8–9

ValueQuest Ltd., 21–22
Venture-capital funds, 46

Wal-Mart, Jack Welch on, 96–97
Walton, Sam, 13

Welch, Jack, interview with, 93–111
Williams, Ella D., 105–106
Wilson, Wendy, 106
W.L. Gore & Associates, 38–39
Women entrepreneurs, 99–106
  financing for, 103–105
  hours worked by, 106
  minority, 105–106
  obstacles faced by, 103–106
  quality of jobs provided by,
    102–103
  as talent pool, 100–101
Workers (*see* Employees)
Working Capital, 50
Workplace, attractiveness of, 68–69

Zabarkes, Rochelle, 104–105
Zeneca PLC, 69
Zynaxis Inc., 64–65

About the Editors

Business Week, a McGraw-Hill company, is the world's
leading business magazine. More than 100 reporters and
editors contributed to this book, which is based on a
special bonus issue of the magazine plus additional
material. *Small Business Trends and Entrepeneurship* is the
second in the *Business Week Guides* series based on these
annual special issues; the first was *The Quality
Imperative*.